For Claudia

Karlheinz Moll

America

Land of unlimited Controversies

The Author
Karlheinz Moll, born 1966 in Meckenbeuren, is a consultant in the international financial service industry. Karlheinz lives in Munich, Germany and is currently working on his first novel.

Bibliography
FATCA – Wenn der Fiskus zweimal klingelt (2014)
Amerika _ Land der unbegrenzten Gegensätze (2015)
America – Land of unlimited controversies (2016)
Ego-Shooter – The Deep of the Pain (2017)

Table of Contents

'Whatever you are, be a good one' – Abraham Lincoln

Introduction

I am roaming through the United States of America for almost 25 years now, was employed by an American bank in Germany for many years and obviously have watched way too many old fashioned Western movies, the way they were produced in the heyday of the genre during the 1940s and 1950s. Enough reasons to not being impressed and influenced by the United States.

When talking to people anywhere around the globe about the United States there is one thing I realized; people either cherish the States, like I do, or completely dislike America. There seems to be very little in between those two poles. The same poles exist within the country itself.

These notions of controversies and disparities are continuously visible everywhere in the country and its people. There is barely an issue, be it politics, religion, the economy or the society, where extreme views, laws, regulations and opposing opinions aren't looming in black and white.

If you are a foreigner to the U.S., you may have heard, seen or experienced numerous cases on your own, on television and in newspapers, stories from family and friends or from own encounters while traveling through the United States on business or leisure.

I have to admit that even my enthusiasm for the United States does not prevent me from experiencing my own set of controversies. For example; I can talk for hours about the seemingly endless beauty of the nature, the special kind of people I have met there and whose optimism, relaxedness and friendliness I can´t praise enough.

On the other hand there are times where I have real difficulties dealing with some of the things that are happening in the American society, especially in politics.

I want to use this book to talk about some of these controversies. The stories and examples are taken from my own memories and encounters, came up during previous or recent discussions or surfaced during the research phase of the book.

Whenever I am talking about America, USA or the States anywhere in this book I am referring to the United States of America. I noticed that most people in the States and here in Europe referring to America as if there were no South, Middle or North America.

Whenever I am talking about Americans, the U.S. population or the People of the United States in more or less general terms I am trying to cover about 80% of the population or some 250 Million people. This still constitutes a strong level of generalization and will certainly not be justifiable and pleasing to anyone but you got to start somewhere.

You will undoubtedly note that the West of the United States, its specialties and history will be overrepresented and in the center of many stories told throughout the chapters as compared to the eastern part of the country and the coastal regions. This is owned to my personal preference for the big skies and vast country of the good ole West with its small towns and long, colorful history.

At some points in the book you may wonder if the author has laid his fingers rather deep in some of the open wounds but you hopefully will find an equal number of positive stories with the goal to somehow provide a balanced impression. I am not sure whether I have always achieved this goal, but believe me, I tried. Outside the United States, which is a lot of territory by the way, many people are often puzzled with issues like gun ownership, death penalty or climate change America seems to struggle with and it appears to the ´Outsiders´ as if Americans would at least sometimes live in a parallel universe or in some version of the Bizarro world from the Superman comics.

On the other hand and despite all criticism America still manages to positively surprise us every now and then. Just like in 2015 with a few breakthrough events, which will have a lasting effect on the U.S., legally, politically and on society in general.

The first event was a legal victory for President Barrack Obama and his signature initiative, the U.S. version of a universal health care. Then there was the decision of the U.S. Supreme Court legalizing homosexual marriages and thus ending a decade long polarizing issue which may still cause sleepless nights in some conservative circles, not limited to county clerks issuing marriage licenses and Ted Cruz.

From a foreign policy point of view some events in 2015 were equally historic. Cuba, which had been a poster-boy enemy for more than 50 years in the American backyard, literally got a handshake from President Barrack Obama. In the meantime, Cuba and the U.S. have both re-opened their consultancies, cruise ships are stopping over, and tourism is picking up the pieces lost before the revolution. Travelers are rushing to book trips because they want to get a glimpse of the old Cuba before Starbucks and McDonalds triggering their friendly takeovers. Collectors of vintage U.S. cars probably can´ t wait shipping U.S. cars from the 1940s and 1950s back to the United States. Public resistance was barely noticeable and even one of the Republican presidential hopefuls, Mr. Rubio, could not benefit from his outrage. The cherry on the cake was the visit of President Obama in Cuba in March 2016. The last American President visiting Cuba was Calvin Coolidge in 1928.

The nuclear deal brokered between the five constant members of the United Nation`s Security Council, China, France, Russia the United Kingdom and the United States plus Germany, and the regime in Iran might end the political ice age and the economic isolation for the former arch enemy. The Presidential race 2016 and the TV debates in particular, also know as political casting shows, may have left millions of Americans wondering if this is just a new scripted reality format. Unfortunately not!

In February 2016 the death of Antonin Scalia, one of the nine judges on the U.S. Supreme Court, started a fierce ideological battle against President Obama, mainly triggered by GOP Presidential hopefuls. Although the U.S. Constitution gives a clear mandate to President Obama, still to be 10 months in office at the time of the death of Judge Scalia, the Republican establishment wants to pull all strings to have the legal process nominating a successor stalled or delayed. The GOP, hoping to win the Presidency in November 2016, understandably, want to replace the late conservative judge Scalia with an equally conservative successor.

As a movie buzz I added selective movie and TV recommendations at the end of most of the chapters. The film and TV show titles to some extent cover the subject of the respective chapter. It is no coincidence that most of the motion pictures and series listed and named are Western. Finally, you may easily notice that English is not my mother tongue. I may speak English quite fairly but still it is a long stretch compared to a native speaker. So please accept my sincere apologies if sentences here and there could need some polishing.

Enjoy the ride!

Part I

Wilderness and Big City Lights

1. Land Distribution

Those among you who had the opportunity to at least once take a trip with a car, motor home, a motor cycle or even on horseback through the United States outside the big cities may remember the sheer endless drives often passing vast and barely inhabited country. During such drives it is easy getting carried away by the beauty of the endless landscape.

The United States including Alaska and Hawaii have a size of 3,794,100 sq. mi or 9.826.675 km² [1] and offer almost any type of geography and topography. Regardless whether you want to go to the mountains or heading to the beach, preferring glaciers over deserts, like rainforest as much as the prairie, all of it and then some can be found in the United States rarely having to cross any border to get there.

The land, regardless if you consider the Viking Leif Erikson somewhere around the year 1,000 AD or rather Christopher Columbus in the year 1492 as the first to ´discover´ what should one day become the United States of America, no later than 1492 the country was meant to belong to the new arrivals. It should be noted that ´belong to´ from back then until the 18th century meant the European kingdoms like England, France,

---

[1] Source: The World Factbook, accessed on January 12, 2015

the Netherlands or Spain. The natives, who roamed and settled the American continent maybe as early as some 13,000 ago was of minor importance from the very beginning, if any at all.

There is a term in the United States that best describes the once untouched and vast landscape; it is called ´Frontier´. It is the name of the wild unknown region beyond the borders of civilization that called for being explored and conquered.

Maybe it was this ´Frontier´ that helped the American people adopting their famous level of enthusiasm and their pragmatic way of taking action as well as optimistically looking into the future, at least back then, and leaving the past behind with no regret and no questions asked. Without these positive attitudes the newcomers may not have succeeded in continuously moving further west beyond what was then known as the frontier.

When browsing through American history books, journals and magazines searching for the places that where once called frontier, different answers are being provided, depending on the year it was written.

Far into the 17th century most of what was called America were more or less the thinly populated regions along the northeastern coastal line what is current day New England. During the first quarter of the 18th century it were trappers and fur traders who followed the tracks of the Delaware and Shawnee Indians on their hunting grounds along the Ohio River[2].

In the following years it were the immigrants from Germany who helped shifting the green border further towards the present Pennsylvania. In the decades after that till the mid of the 19th century it were the borders of the states of Nebraska and Kansas that were considered the frontier.

After the Civil War the westward settlement of the parts of the land what could, to some extent, still be called wild or unconquered, accelerated with high speed. Around 1880 there was not much left on the North American continent that could still be called ´Frontier´.

Movie Recommendations:
- *Last of the Mohicans starring Daniel Day Lewis*
- *Mohawk starring Scott Brady*
- *Far Horzizon starring Fred MacMurray*
- *Unconquered starring Gary Cooper*

---

[2] Source: Frederick Jackson Turner: The Significance of the Frontier in American History (1893), accessed on June 15, 2015

2. Land of the Free

The end of the Revolutionary War, also known as the War of Independence from 1775 to 1783 between the former 13 American colonies on one side and Great Britain on the other side marked the beginning of a far reaching distribution of land given to the people who already populated the young nation or immigrated from Europe that lasted for almost 200 years.

The newly formed United States of America only ´owned´ a small portion of the landscape it is today but the distribution of the vast parts of the land in possession started after the last bullet was fired and the gun smoke on the battle fields faded away.

Initially land distribution was an inexpensive way of compensating veterans who fought for independence in the Revolution. The Land Act of 1796 probably was the first land distribution law of the new nation. Later on, the governmental organized distribution of land became a probate instrument in the settlement policy.

Some of the more prominent examples are the Indian Removal Act of 1830 or the Homestead Act of 1862. The first one was signed into law by President Andrew Jackson to rid of the civilized tribes of the Chickasaw, Choctaw, Creek, Muscogee Creek and Seminole from their traditional homeland in the South East of the United States and which reached its humanitarian low with the 'Trail of Tears'. The second one became law under President Abraham Lincoln in the midst of the Civil War and meant to create an opportunity for veterans and freed slaves. More coverage on these two politically motivated initiatives will follow later on.

The taking of the land in the years after the American Civil War caused quite a few disputes between settlers who considered themselves proud owners of a nice parcel of allocated land and descendants of Spanish conquistadores, who, at least in some cases, were heirs of even older land distributions, so called Spanish land grants dating back to a time when states like Texas or California belonged to the Spanish crown.

There were cases back then, where Spanish aristocrats and noblemen went to court or took a short cut by visiting the Rancher or Farmer directly and presented them with a document that looked like a Spanish land grant from the 17th or 18th century. The people who considered themselves as the rightful owners of the parcel of land and who cultivated it learned that their land was now reclaimed by the offspring of a colonial, Spanish nobleman.

In most of these cases the new settlers were able to have the upper hand, as quite often the alleged documents issued by the Spanish crown were in fact forgeries. But some of the Spanish claims were valid and the newcomers from the East had to leave the land distributed to them. To this day there are land owners in California and other states who own vast tracks of land as a result of Spanish land grants.

But there was no reason for too many worries. Space and free land was available plentiful, at least back then. Settlers and adventurers acquired and secured, other might say took and occupied, the conquered territory.

'The first hundred years it was the task of the United States to take possession of the land' concluded the lawyer Sheldon Green[3]. In fact, over a billion acres[4], or 400 million hectares of land were granted, sold or simply given away during the first hundred years since the founding of the United States of America.

Movie Recommendations:
- *Seminola starring Rock Hudson*
- *The President's Lady starring Charlton Heston*

---

[3] Source: Taking back our land: A History of Railroad Grant Reform, George Draffan, 1998

[4] Source: U.S. Bureau of Land Management

3. Trains on a Checkerboard

While war veterans were the main benefactors of land grants in the late 18th century, it were the large railroad companies which got their hands on huge tracks of land during the first half of the 19th century.

To motivate the large conglomerates and building companies, which were needed to build the railroads, laying tracks and telegraph lines, in particular the transcontinental railroad from east to west straight to the Pacific, these companies received considerable land grants. Otherwise it would had been difficult convincing these firms laying railroad tracks, especially without any economic outlook and guaranties.

The railroad companies were offered between 6 and 40 Miles, or between 10 and 64 km to the left and to the right of the tracks. The government considered these grants as kind of payment and these companies were free to either sell or use the land. It was also meant as another motivational move to ensure high quality railroad connections were built instead of just throwing miles of tracks into the prairie.

As it was expected that the settlement and the economic development of the west would blossom along the railroad tracks, it seemed like a pretty good initiative at first. In total, more than one million acres of land were granted to the railroad companies alone and some of these companies or its succeeding organizations belong to the largest property owners in the United States to this day.

To prevent that those large, continuous and enormous parts of the country would end up in the hands of the railroad companies and to also profit from the development of the land, the Government invented a new system for the distribution of land, simply called Checkerboard[5].

The land along the planned path for the railroad tracks was divided into quadrants of 640 acres each and numbered. The quadrants with the uneven numbers were allocated to the railroad companies and the Government kept the parcels with the even numbers.

The plans of the Government included selling ´their´ parcels to foreign immigrants, who were highly welcome back then, and citizens willing to settle in the vast, almost inhibited country. However, the parcels were too large so that the majority of the poor masses could not afford it, whereas the affluent Americans in the east had little interest acquiring land in the middle of nowhere.

In relation to the general price developments of rural property aimed for agriculture, cattle or settlement, raw checker boarded land previously owned by the Government or railroad companies in scarcely populated

---

[5] Source: Wikipedia, Checkerboarding, accessed on January 13, 2015

regions of Nevada, South Dakota or Wyoming are available today for quite affordable prices. Potential buyers, who are interested in owning their piece of the American West, can select properties of many hundred acres or more.

A property with 160 acres may be available for less than USD 200 an acre. Of course buyers need to accept that such parcels of raw land are mostly several or even many miles away from what could be called civilization. Another factor to consider is that such investments are not suitable for so called flippers, meaning selling a property shortly after buying it. If you buy checker boarded land somewhere in the west, it might be that you have to wait many years to realize a decent profit or to find a seller on short notice.

A reason for that is the limited number of potential buyers and sellers in that selective niche of the real estate business. However, those who add patience as a characteristic to potential buyers of raw land can expect a nice, though no overwhelming gain of property value.

The value of the land increases at least by the inflation rate and prices almost never fall. You may call it an inflation protected investment not meant for speculation or as Will Rogers once put it 'Don't wait to buy land, buy land and wait'.

The railroad companies were very successful in making economic use of the checker board quadrants allocated to them, in many ways. Through continuous land grants the big railroad companies were able to increase their land ownerships and could keep competitors at distance. The rail road conglomerates sometimes also managed to slow the settlement of certain regions to drive up the price of land.

Another aspect was and is to this very day that many quadrants include economically profitable, harvestable forests or that are adjacent to National Parks. The Government in quite a few cases had to raise large sums to repurchase checker boarded parcels bordering National Parks. Not seldom these parcels had little economic value for the owners in stark contrast to the Government who is still interested increasing existing parks, like the Glacier Park in Montana.

Movie Recommendations:
- *Union Pacific starring Joel McCrea*
- *Western Union starring Randolph Scott*

4. Home Sweet Home

While the American Civil War was still ravaging between the Blue and the Grey with no end in sight, President Abraham Lincoln signed the Homestead Act in 1862, granting 160 acres of land to any person willing to settle on the allocated land and committed to farm or ranch the property for at least 5 years in order to keep it.

The initiative of Abraham Lincoln was not without political motivation. At a time where the Confederate States were fighting to keep their slaves, among other reasons, the North wanted to give land to former slaves. Even women (!) were allowed to receive a parcel. What a symbol for individual freedom.

There were further initiatives of land distribution in the years after the Civil War which were all somewhat based on the original Homestead Act. One of those initiatives was to increase the land grants over time from originally 160 acres up to finally 640 acres.

Some of the land distribution laws that more or less were loosely based on the Homestead Act expired no earlier than 1986. During the prime time of the land grants some 270 million acres of land or 10% of the landscape of the continuous United States were distributed to about 1.6 million willing settlers in the years till 1934[6].

Like the land grants to the railroad companies the Homestead Act had its downsides. The distribution of land opened the door for massive fraud. This was particularly true for land grants with large tracts of grass land or where water was plentiful.

Ranchers, particularly those on the open range, required ever larger tracts of land and enough water for the thousands of head of cattle. Land grants under the Homestead Act were the perfect opportunity to acquire large continuous tracts of land for a bargain price, some might say literally for free.

Because of the very long distances from ranch and farm land in the west to governmental agencies in the east, which would had been able to detect any misuse of land grants, ranchers and increasingly large scale farmers had no problems using con schemes with ′men of straw′ to get a grip on more land.

After the five years required for the land grantee to fully own the land granted were over, the ′men of straw′ could officially sell the land to the very person who in reality possessed it already during these years. Very few of such schemes were ever detected which should be no surprise.

---

[6] Source: National Archives, www.archives.gov, accessed on January 26, 2015

There were plenty of cases were elected public servants were involved in such lucrative deals.

Movie Recommendations:
- *How the West was won starring John Wayne*
- *Woman of Straw starring Sean Connery*

5. Indians on a Checkerboard

The Indians, for political correctness currently also called Native Americans could not escape the checker board system. Large tracts of land that were once the hunting grounds for many Indian tribes, at least prior to the arrival of the white man, were subdivided under the checker board system.

It is understandable that the Indians did not like it much having their traditional lands split and ´interrupted´ by land tracts that were once theirs and were now to be settled by the white men. At least the checker boarding was not as bad as previous Indian removal campaigns.

The most infamous and probably most sad chapter was the Indian Removal Act of 1830. As the name indicates, the act was about the removal, forcefully if needed, of the Indians who lived and were spread out in the territories of what is Florida and Georgia today.

It should be noted that the tribes that lived in Florida and Georgia in the 1830s like the Cherokee, Chickasaw or Seminole had quite some time ago adapted much to the white man´s lifestyle. They farmed and cultivated their land; many sent their children to public schools and wore the same clothes as their fellow pale faces.

To no avail! The man in the White House back then, President Andrew Jackson was the leading force behind the removal law while others like Davy Crockett, who later fought and died at the Alamo, strongly opposed the initiative. The act and its cruel implications are one of the reasons that some would like to see Andrew Jackson being removed from the 10 Dollar bill.

One important reason for the relocation of the Indians was that the white plantation owners in the South needed space for their cotton to grow and for their slaves to pick it.

The act intended the removal of ten thousands of Indians of several tribes and to settle them in current day Oklahoma. If does not require a degree in geography to understand that Oklahoma is a completely different country as Georgia or Florida. But that is not something politicians and land speculators were worrying much about. At least President Andrew Jackson promised that the new land should be theirs forever.

The Seminoles were pretty much the only tribe back then who not only opposed the removal, they also refused to go and with much success. They moved deep into the swamp lands of Florida, the Everglades. This way they were able to keep the moving company aka the U.S. Army at a distance for many years until the Government resonated and the Seminoles could remain in Florida.

The other tribes were not that lucky. In the years after the law was enacted the Indians had to start the hardened march to Oklahoma, watched by the Cavalry to ensure every soul got on its way. The march made history as 'Trail of Tears', because thousands died by hunger, illness and deceases on the long trail[7].

Those who survived and arrived in Oklahoma took years to adapt to the new and strange land, but they managed to farm the land that they were told to be theirs forever as much as they did back in their homeland.

'Forever' though did not last very long. In the years after the Civil War it was time to call the movers again and relocate to territories that were far less inhabitable than where they were now. On the downside too was that the new reservations were much smaller than the current ones. But, again, they were told it would last as long as the water flows and the grass grows.

The Dawes Act of 1878[8], named after the Senator Henry Dawes brought an end of the Government's previous handling of the Indians. In the years prior to 1870 it were primarily military campaigns, removals and deportations into reservations that were used to make room for the never ending stream of the white man into almost every corner of the continent.

---

[7] Source: Gloria Jahoda: The Trail of Tears, 1995

[8] Source: http://www.ourdocuments.gov/doc.php?flash=true&doc=50, accessed on January 13, 2015

The Dawes Act tried something new. The act for the first time wanted to give land to the Indians instead of taking it away from them. Every Native individually should get between 40 and 160 Acres in the checker board system. The fact that Indians with their tradition of common ownership and tribal culture had little use for individual land ownership was once again of little importance.

The Government seemed really to believe that all Indians, who would adapt to the lifestyle of the pale faces, would be less dependent on social welfare and would prosper much better than they ever could in a reservation. So they took some of the reservations, subdivided it and distributed the parcels individually.

Unfortunately, others may say as expected, the whole initiative rarely bore any success. Most parcels that were allocated to Indians were pure raw tracts of land which mostly were useless for ranching or farming and also worthless for almost anything else. However, it was no longer worthless once gold was discovered on Indian land.

On checker boarded land distributed to Indians where gold was found it typically did not take much time to find a reason to call to arms. In the end the long knives or blue coats had to be called in to remove the red man from the gold fields. In the end the Indians also had to leave much of the land that was so well intended given to them.

Remember the stubborn Seminoles, who fought so hard to stay in Florida? For them playing hard ball with the U.S. Government worked out just fine over time The Seminoles are one of the economically most successful tribes in the United States.

The Seminoles were among the first tribes that started a successfully venture in the gaming industry. In the years after 1979 the Seminoles built and operated the first casinos across their reservation. A further important milestone was the acquisition of the restaurant chain ´Hard Rock Café´.[9]

Movie Recommendations:
- *The White Feather starring Robert Wagner*
- *Cheyenne starring Richard Widmark*
- *Broken Arrow starring James Stewart*

---

[9] Source: Wikipedia, Keyword: Seminole, accessed on August 3, 2015

6. Straw Men playing Checkerboard

Only a few may be really surprised to hear that the enormous distribution of land ownership from governmental into private hands lured numerous crooks to the game.

The distributed land was so far away from Washington and law and order that those interested in much more land than they were allowed to obtain could use all tricks at their disposal to get a larger piece of the pie.

Besides classic land speculators who simply wanted to acquire land to profit from price increases and selling it later on to land hungry settlers it were the railroad companies as well as large land owners who looked for ways to get more land than they were legally entitled to.

Very often it were parcels next to each other which were targeted for fraudulent ventures. Men of straw were plentiful and could easily be motivated to act as buyers of land parcels which they would then immediately resell to parties that were really interested in the land, or, if the land distribution was linked to a minimum waiting and holding period of up to 5 years at least tried to work the property on paper they were supposed to own.

It may had been legal but certainly not morally sound when owners of a parcel of land ensured that their children and grandparents could get a hold on adjoining parcels. This way the total land ownership could be increased substantially, remembering that people had a lot of children back then. One or two generations later the grandchildren and their grandchildren inherited those parcels. Those way whole regions were once owned by family clans.

Corruption among politicians and bribes to public servants were not uncommon to circumvent the rules for land distribution and grants. There were occasions were land was simply taken away from rightful owners by using every legal trick in the book, stealing the land might be a better term describing it.

At the beginning of the 20th century the state of Oregon had cases of fraud where more than a thousand people were indicted and ended up in front of a judge in the years between 1903 and 1910. Among those charged more than a hundred were lawyers, surveyors and even Senators and House Representatives. On the other hand, there were not that many incidents as the uncounted number of Westerns telling land grabbing stories may want us to believe.

Movie Recommendations:
-   *Once a time in the West starring Charles Bronson*

7. Hare and Hedgehog in Cimarron

One of the last distributions of vast chunks of land occurred at the end of the 19th century in parts of what was soon to be a former Indian Reservation in Oklahoma. In 1889, the Indian Appropriation Bill, in other words a land distribution regulation, was changed in a way that President Benjamin Harrison could release 2 million acres of land ready for settlement.

Behind the cute name 'Indian Appropriation Bill' was another initiative of the U.S. Government to relocate Indians from their current Reservation, which were once given to the tribes forever, and settle them in much less attractive, to spare the word inhabitable, parts of the country. Even back then the U.S. Government seemed to be masters in covering cruel measures with fancy names and meaningless words.

In practice, the often heard and given promises to Indians 'As long as the grass grows and the water flows' probably translated into something like 'As long as we don't have another use for the land or someone else wants it'.

In 1889 the Homestead Act of 1862 was still in effect and under the Indian Appropriation Bill every motivated settler who would claim one of the available parcels and register it would own a piece of the American dream or as Mark Twain put it 'Buy land...they don't make it anymore'.

The 'Land Run', as this special type of land distribution was also called was one of a kind in the American history. You did not have to mail in a request. You did not have to ask anybody. You only had to be physically present on April 22, 1889 and get in line along the Oklahoma state lines bordering Arkansas and Texas on feet, on horseback, by carriage or wagon, rain or shine.

The interested parties of land hungry settlers, spectators and claim jumpers alike gathered in the town of Guthrie. The then tiny township which could barely be found on any map prior to the Land Run, even today has a very small population of about 1,000. Harper's Weekly summarized it perfectly by saying 'In contrast to Rome Guthrie was built in one day'[10].

A shot from a gun signaled the start of the Land Run. You have to picture it like today when a big electronic company introduces its latest gadget like a tablet or smart phone. You probably have seen the pictures on many occasions where buyers camp in front of the entrance and then, as soon as the store opens, they are storming the store like vandals to get that piece of merchandise as if where the last one available on earth and if there would be no tomorrow.

---

[10] Source: Harper's Weekly 33, May 18, 1889, accessed on January 20, 2015

The land run in Oklahoma 1889 had its own dynamic and flaws. Everyone that headed on had an own idea which might be the best parcel to aim for. Regardless what they had in mind, the best parcels were often claimed already when they arrived at the parcel of their desire, although the arrivers, some of them on racing horses, could swear be up front without any chasers but still seemed to be too slow and thus too late.

The truth behind the mystery was massive fraud. It was like the ´Hare and the Hedgehog´ game. Obviously, a lot of people entered the distributable land way before the starting shot, sometimes even camped out there days before and occupied the parcel they desired.

When the first land seekers arrived they just needed to act as if they started with the others and just managed to be faster than all the others. Most of those losing out obviously did not ask the ´winners´ how they managed to be there faster on foot or on a donkey than those on horseback.

The cavalry had tried to block off the distributable land to prevent that people would enter the territory before the starting shot. That was wishful thinking and the reality was far from that. It is said that 9 out of 10 of the parcels of land that were available in the Land Run of 1889 were acquired illegally and fraudulently.

There were some more illegal land grabbing activities in the close vicinity although of different nature and caused by a legal loophole. For a short period of time after the Civil War the Cimarron Strip in the Oklahoma Panhandle was called 'No man's land'. Background for this grey zone of legal uncertainty was unclear zoning between the Reservation of the Cherokee and the United States.

After a while the strip was allocated to the Oklahoma Territory. During the time the loophole existed thousands of illegal land claims and settlements occurred. But land that did not belong to anybody could not be taken away from anybody. Land spectators had a field day.

However the strip of the so called 'No man's land' never was a place without any law even though the movie industry picked up the story and produced a bunch of Western films during the 1940s and 1950s that played with the idea, that the territory was a place where lawless people could hide and live peacefully without being disturbed by the law.[11]

Movie Recommendations:
- *Last of the Bad Men starring Robert Ryan*
- *Cimarron (1931) starring Richard Dix*
- *Cimarron (1960) starring Glenn Ford*
- *Bad Man's Territory starring Randolph Scott*

---

[11] Source: Wikipedia, Oklahoma Panhandle, accessed on January 27, 2015.

8. Once upon a time in Montana

I guess I already mentioned that I am a big fan of the American West. My favorite place is the state of Montana. The Big Sky state and its second largest city Missoula, despite its population of just about 70,000, are among the best examples for the beauty and wide open spaces the United States have to offer.

Montana has a size of 380.000 square kilometers, which is about the size of Germany but the state of Montana has a population of about 1 million compared to 80 million in Germany on roughly the same size of land. That relates to only 2.5 people per square kilometer in Montana while there are 226 people per square kilometer in Germany.

The whole state of Montana has an almost overwhelming piece of nature to offer. Earlier sins against nature, like the massive logging or the paper production made place for an El Dorado of outdoor activities, not limited to the Yellowstone Park being one of the most popular National Parks in the south east of Montana or the Glacier Park in the north sharing the border with Canada.

The city of Missoula was built in the midst of a valley surrounded by rolling, grassy hills. In summer the grass on these hills dries out and turns the spring green into a yellowish look. The summers in the last couple of years had been pretty hot and the winters are not as cold and snowy as they used to be. The climate change has left its footprint. However, higher up in the mountains winter still brings plenty of snow for winter sports.

Missoula is a university city of international reputation, a bit like the Heidelberg of America comes to my mind, where the world seems still to be in order and where a small town atmosphere provides a feeling of coziness.

The University is the biggest employer of the city of Missoula. Parents from around the globe are sending their offspring to Missoula to study at a place where their children get both, a high level of education and challenging curriculum as well as a perceived safe place outside the big cities and an abundant nature that offers enough room for activities, be it wild water rafting, fly fishing or snowboarding.

Normally, Missoula barely makes it into the headlines as not much dramatic is happening there that would get viewer´s attention between two commercial breaks. What goes for the United States applies even more to other countries. On the international scene there were even less occasions to report anything about the whereabouts of Missoula. With two exceptions that are equally notable and sad.

The first case goes back more than 70 years. After the Japan attack on Pearl Harbor and the entry of the United States into World War II thereafter some extreme measures were taken regarding immigrants and U.S.

Citizens who or whose ancestors originated from countries now at war with the United States.

At times about thousand people, mostly men of Japanese and Italian descent, were captured in Fort Missoula. Back then Fort Missoula, as most of Montana, was still a secluded place that still had its flair of the old frontier times. The fact of being far away from the ´Outer World´ bared little risks that those people kept in Fort Missoula would somehow be able establishing contact to the enemy. Not that the people held there intended that.

Most of the people were U.S. Citizens or immigrated to the United States long ago. But these were times of war. The trauma after the attack on Pearl Harbor still was on the people´s minds and the American type of paranoia could prevail just as it did again after 9/11.

The second time Missoula made headlines happened only recently. A student from Germany, who also enjoyed studying in Missoula, was shot after entering a garage of a home, obviously trying to lift a can of beer. What may have at first sounded like a normal but stupid attempt of theft became a drama after a second and closer look. In the midst of this tragic event was once more a gun and a person overeager to use it.

As already mentioned, Missoula is far from being a town for party hungry students. For those who are out for some nightly entertainment, there is not much of a club and bar scene. Some of those looking for some late night action came up with the strange 'game' of 'garage hopping', meaning breaking and entering into other people's garages and stealing their beer. Getting bored is one thing, getting criminal another. Maybe this type of leisure 'sport' has lost some of its attraction after the recent events.

It is understandable that home owners want to protect their garages and what's in it. A good and probate trick to keep intruders away would be to close and lock the garage. At least one garage owner thought differently and had his own idea of dealing with the students. He did exactly the opposite what a person would do protecting his property.

He left the garage door open, installed a motion detector and the trap was set. Once the student from Germany detected the open garage door and wanted to grab some cans of beer, the home owner greeted him with a rifle and shot him straight through the garage door. Just like in the old Wild West manner of shooting first and asking questions later. It remains unknown if the homeowner asked anything at all as the German student died on the spot from the spray of bullets.

During the trial it was said that the shooter was setting a trap and shot the student as he would have been on a hunting trip. The jury came in with a guilty verdict and the prison sentence was much harder as generally expected.

It was also interesting to see that the call of the gun lobby for the right of self-defense was turned down by the worries of the public regarding the safety of their children. We will talk about gun ownership and the self-defense debate in more depth later on in this book.

It would now be rather sad talking so much about a great city like Missoula, a place I call among my favorites in the Unites States and where there are countless reasons to come and visit, and not having more to tell about it than those cruel stories. With that on my mind you will find some more stories coming up in the next chapter that are somewhat connected to Montana and Missoula which at least have a happy ending.

Movie Recommendations:
- *Legends of the Fall starring mit Brad Pitt*
- *A River runs through starring Brad Pitt*

9. Tatanka and Buffalo Bill

L ike many countries too, the United States got a few animals that pose as national symbols or heraldic animals. Some of the best known animals that are so very typical for America are Buffalo or Bison, very often called America Buffalo. The name Buffalo derives from the French word ′Le Boeuf′ used by trappers.

Maybe you remember the now classic ′Dancing with Wolves′ starring Kevin Costner who also directed the epic movie. In the movie the Lakota Indians called Buffalo Tatanka. Tatanka is Sioux language and means something like ′Bull Buffalo′. Going deeper into the terminology the literal translation from the Lakota language Tatanka means ′He who owns us′[12].

Today′s bison go back about 5,000 years and are descendants of an ancient bison race that roamed the earth some 2 million years ago. It is estimated that around the year 1800 up to 60 million bison wandered the prairies of North America. The arrival of the White Man in the American West and the settlement in the prairie states of the USA started the almost complete extinction of these impressive animals.

---

[12] Source: tatankafund.org, accessed on May 12, 2015

The bison were hunted and slaughtered in large quantities. First the railroad workers needed meat and the buffalo offered plenty of it. During that time the buffalo hunter William Frederick Cody 'earned' his nick name 'Buffalo Bill'. Good Buffalo hunters were able to kill a 100 or more animals a day. Next were the ranchers who needed space for their hundreds of thousands head of cattle.

In the end it was political maneuvers which almost caused the complete extinction of the Buffalo. During the Indian wars the cavalry started to systematically shoot down every Buffalo herd they could find. Every dead Buffalo meant less food for the Indians. Starving the Indians was a very effective way solving the Indian 'problem'.

The initiator of this war strategy was General Phil Sheridan, who after the Civil War obviously did not have enough of fighting so he looked for new war territories. Sheridan let the military campaigns against the Cheyenne, Comanche and Kiowa and used the bison as a weapon against the Indians.

History has it that he told the Comanche chief Tosawi in 1869 that the only good Indians he ever met were dead ones. Later on this was translated into the now infamous sentence 'Only a dead Indian is a good Indian' that were used in so many Western movies[13].

---

[13] Source: Wikipedia: 'Phil Sheridan', accessed on July 15, 2015

The slaughtering of the Buffalos reduced the population to about 5.5 million around 1870[14]. At the turn from the 19th to the 20th century only a few hundred of these mighty animals survived. With the population so low, the few ones left did not really disturb anyone anymore and with the Indians all put up in Reservations it was time for a new thinking. Protecting the nature and animals were not high on the priority list of the people in the early years of the 20th century but a shift of mind was visible.

In 1908 the National Bison Range was established close to St. Ignatius, roughly an hour north of Missoula. The park has a size of 18,800 Acres where up to 500 bison roam today. In the years until after World War II the Bison Range and other parks increased the population back to more than 5,000 animals.

Another very good example is a Bison reservation on 31,000 Acres in the vicinity of Bozeman, Montana. Bozeman is settled east of Missoula half way to the biggest city in Montana, Billings. In this reservation the ´American Prairie Reserve´ project was started in 2005 with 16 bison, which were brought there from the Wind Cave National Park. The herd has grown to 440 animals in 2015.

By 2018 it is expected that the bison population in the reservation will reach 1,000. In addition to the natural reproduction animals from other herds are mixed with the population in the reservation for greater diversi-

---

[14] Source: Wikipedia, American Buffalo, accessed on May 05, 2015

ty. The project aims towards 10,000 Buffalo in 2028 which would then be the largest herd in the United States, even more than the 5,000 animals wandering through the Yellowstone Park.

The project put up fences around the Reservation. The idea is not to keep the Bison in the Reservation or to keep other wild animals out. The main reason is simply to keep the biggest intruder at bay; the ones on two legs packing heat. The reservation is open though for guided excursions and (unarmed) nature watching[15].

Further south in Utah there is another important and well known reservation for Buffalo. What makes this one special is that the bison are located on an island. In 1893, a few frontier guys with business on their mind took 12 animals and shipped them to Antelope Island just an hour from Salt Lake City. On one hand they wanted to protect some of the last Bison, on the other hand they wanted to use the island as a hunting ground.[16]

The idea was to offer hunters a place where they still could hunt buffalo for a hefty fee. In 1926 they charged USD 300 to shoot a Buffalo, which today would be USD 4,000. But that is long gone. Today the reserve hosts 775 bison. Every year the park offers a weekend for city slick-

---

[15] Source: American Prairie Reserve, 2014 Bison Report

[16] Source: New York Times, Antelope Island, October 26, 2015

ers when the Bison are rounded up and vaccinated. Some of them are sold and slaughtered to keep the population growth healthy.

In total there are about 500,000 American Buffalo in private hands and more than 30,000 animals on public lands across the United States. It is a proof what is possible, when the will of the society, business and politics meet in harmony and are put to work.

Movie Recommendations:
- *The Last Hunt starring Stewart Granger*
- *Dances with Wolves starring Kevin Costner*
- *The White Buffalo starring mit Charles Bronson*

10.   The luck on Horseback...

Similar to the American Buffalo, horses, particularly Mustangs are ´symbolic´ animals of the United States. Horses, though not exactly the ones we know today, existed in the U.S. for a few million years. However, those species extinct after the last ice age about 12,000 years ago. Scientists assume that the arrival of the first humans who migrated from Asia to America had a lot to do with it.

Mustangs, derived from Spanish, are quite often called wild horses, but they are not. Correctly, it could be said ´horses gone wild´. Mustangs are descendants from horses which the Spanish conquistadors under Cortés brought to the then New World from 1519 onwards.

For the next 300 years many of those horses escaped, were sold or were left by the Spaniards once they withdrew from America and Mexico. Over the years the originally tamed horses were literally ´gone wild´ and in the almost unpopulated wilderness the band of animals turned into impressive herds.

Horses played an important ´supporting´ role in the attempts of the humans to conquer and settle the American West, be it the Indians who wandered over the prairie with their mustangs till late in the 18th century, the first white pioneers and trappers or, in later years, the settlers, who in large wagon trains moved west from St. Louis.

Last but not least there were the Pony Express riders, who, during the short time the service operated, rode over vast distances to deliver mail from St. Louis to Sacramento, before the telegraph lines were built putting an end to this extraordinary venture. It is said, thus not proven, that 'Buffalo Bill' was riding for the Pony Express before he changed careers and started earning his nick name as Buffalo hunter and later on starting a career in show business.

At its peak there might had been up to 2 million mustangs that roamed between the deserts of New Mexico and the mountains of Montana. The growth of the population and the relative freedom the horses enjoyed with very few enemies around came to a halt once the westward expansion of the United States came in full swing, leaving less and less space for the mustangs.

Like the buffalo the number of horses went down drastically, particularly once the animals lost their roles as working and transporting animals. In 1959 the Wild Horse Annie Act[17] was passed which became the first law for the protection of mustangs and wild donkeys, which are also called burros. The protective law paved the way for establishing wild horse reservations for the mustangs and burros in several states across the west. Today, some of the largest wild horse reservations are located in Nevada.

---

[17] Source: Wikipedia, Mustangs, accessed on June 03, 2015

A lot of tamed and working horses also did not need to worry too much about new employment opportunities. From the early days of the 20th century Hollywood offered new jobs for horses in the movie industry, primarily Western. Western, certainly the most American of all movie genres, helped shaping the movie production industry and turned Hollywood into the center of film making.

One of the first movie ´hits´ in the early years of film making, ´The Great Train Robbery´ shot in 1903, was a Western. Horses became an important part of the movie industry from the first Western films and it remained that way for the next 100 years. Some horses even became movie stars and their names were equally famous as those of their riders.

Do you remember Champion (Gene Autry), Trigger (Roy Rogers), Silver (Clayton – The Lone Ranger – Moore), Tarzan (Ken Maynard), White Flash (Tex Ritter) or Koko (Rex Allen)? No? There is no reason to worry; these are names from another time, when B-Western movies in good black-and-white with singing cowboys and their well trained horses were part of the weekly Saturday matinee.

Today, Western movies and TV series, putting aside recent exceptions like ´The Homesman´, ´Hell on Wheels´ or ´The Hateful Eight´, are no longer in high demand in the movie industry. However, horses do not feel the need to complain, waiting for unemployment checks or standing in line for food stamps.

Horses are still very popular these days in many parts of America. They belong to households like cats and dogs with the difference or course that they do not live in the house but in the corral. If you happen to take a car trip on country roads, like driving from Portland, Oregon, through Nevada, Idaho and Montana to Cheyenne, Wyoming you will note that there is barely a ranch, settlement or village without noticing plenty of horses on green pastures along the roadside.

The care and the protection of the mustang in the reservations let to an increased population of more than 30,000 horses and 6,000 burros today, distributed in more than 200 herds[18]. Most of them can be found in Nevada, Utah and Wyoming. This level of care comes with a price tag. Currently the maintenance of all the herds in the animal reservations cost USD 75 million each year. From my point of view, every cent of it is well spent.

At times in the 20th century not all horses were always that lucky. Since the 1970s it is illegal to hunt and capture mustangs and send them to the slaughter houses. But still today thousands of them are captured by the authorities and sold because ranchers view the horses as a plague who feed on the pastures they need for their cattle.

But even for those being sold, the sun keeps on shining, at least for some though. For example, if they end up in the Mustang Monument, a

---

[18] Source: Bureau of Land Management (BLM), Wild Horse & Burro Program

private ranch of 2,500 square kilometers in the North East of Nevada called home for more 700 mustangs today[19].

Movie Recommendations:

- *Bite the Bullet starring mit Gene Hackman*
- *Open Range starring Kevin Costner*
- *Wild Horses starring Charles Bronson*
- *The Undefeated starring John Wayne*

[19] Source: Der Stern, issue March 19, 2015

11.   What happens in Vegas...

How do we manage the leap from the wide open spaces and the rural parts of America to urbanity and the cities? A chapter about Las Vegas may do the trick and to build the bridge in the story line. In fact, it sometimes only takes a few minutes by car outside the city limits to feel like being time warped into the good old West.

When you leave Sin City and head north on Mount Charleston Road, a short trip of 25 minutes takes you from the desert high up into the mountains. In winter there is even skiing there. On top of Mount Charleston you might rather feel being in Yosemite Park instead on top of a mountain surrounded by nothing but desert.

Once you are heading back to town on the same road the skyline of Las Vegas will accompany you all the way and when you are in the heart of the gambling city, the exact opposite from what you just experienced is awaiting you.

There is barely any big city in America where it deems appropriate to leave behind, at least during the short time of being there, some of your upbringing and morals as soon you pass the famous welcome street sign at the edge of the town. It is pretty much the same as going to Disney World, just that Las Vegas is mainly meant for adults.

Las Vegas has a very illustrious and interesting history behind it and probably more of that in the years to come. The first structures were erected in the middle of the 19th century and for a long time it was nothing more than a small, sleepy settlement in the desert. A stop-over for people on their trip farther west, be it covered wagons, trains or automobiles.

It would probably have stayed that way if the state of Nevada would not have legalized gambling in 1931. It did not cause much of an attention at first as barely anyone lived in Nevada back then and tourism was not a big issue just yet.

It all started to change when the Family arrived in town to settle down. Unfortunately it was not the type of family with papa, mama, children and a dog but the organized kind, very often with deep Italian roots. In 1945 one of the large families from the east coast sent Bugsy Siegel to the then innocent city. Bugsy Siegel laid the foundation for the future gambling town when he opened the Flamingo hotel and casino.

Unfortunately he could not hold on to his job as local representative of the big investors from Chicago and New York. In 1947 Bugsy Siegel died of heavy lead poising[20]. It is said he had some disputes with the members of the family councils with the names of Lucky Luciano and Meyer Lansky, and you know how dramatic family twists may end up sometimes.

---

[20] Source: Steve Fischer: When the Mob ran Vegas

In the following years, further casinos, like the Sands, the Stardust, the Sahara or the Tropicana were added to the Strip. Those and other hotels and casinos that opened up in Las Vegas were mostly owned and operated by the various ´families´. In the 1950s music and entertainment were added to lure more and more gambling tourist to town. Frank Sinatra and members of his Rat Pack, among them Dean Martin and Sammy Davis Jr., were regular show acts in the Flamingo, the Sands and other venues.

Somewhere between the 1970s and the 1980s, hard to tell the exact dates, the organized family ventures disappeared. Demographics, longer stays in federal facilities or the already mentioned family feuds were the main causes that the mob lost its grip on the town. The hotels and casinos turned into large conglomerates and many of them are listed on the stock exchange today.

For a short while during the 1980s the popularity of Las Vegas was waning. Gambling lost some of its allure and the Rat Pack, once the hottest ticket in town, were playing the harps up in heaven or elsewhere. The change came with places like the Mirage.

The Mirage was the first modern resort hotel and casino that was built on the strip and the hotel hired Siegfried & Roy as entertainment attraction. Shortly after the Treasure Island, Luxor and New York, New York were erected. This adult version of Disney Land lured visitors back to town and gambling in Sin City became very popular again.

Ten years later, further change came to town while the income and revenue from gambling slowly turned south again. It were the resort business, concert attractions and conventions which proofed to be real money-making machines. In the wake of this new boom the Bellagio, where the fountains move to music, the Mandalay Bay, Paris and the Venetian were built, adding thousands of bedrooms on the Strip.

With the same alluring concept in mind, the Aria, the Vdara or the Cosmopolitan were further additions in the last couple of years to the roster of top places to stay in town, the longer the better. Las Vegas may still be the Sin City, but hotel accommodation and food very often have turned into a first class experience.

There is not much left of the classic casinos with smoke smothered gambling halls, female waitresses in very short skirts and cheap buffets. Instead there are star studded restaurants with indecently high prices, entertainers from the top of the list, like Celine Dion or Shania Twain. Some of the newer hotels have separated the lobby from the casino, like the Cosmopolitan, so you do not have to pull your luggage between black jack or roulette tables to get to the elevator.

Technology has also kept pace with these developments. Lightning and sound try to motivate you to spend as much time and money as possible while you are inside the compound. Cameras are following you each step of the way as soon as you enter a casino.

An average casino has well up to 3,000 cameras installed, at times that translates into more than one camera per visitor[21]. Almost nothing remains unwatched. Face recognition software is widely installed to identify gamblers counting cards or are too drunk to keep on loosing money. Even the bars use modern technology now to prevent too much of the valuable liquor ending up in the throats of the bartenders or staff taking it home by the bottle.

The Mandalay Bay operates one of those huge bars practically open all night high in the upper floor of the hotel with great views over the Las Vegas skyline. The bar uses RFID (Radio Frequency ID) technology to manage the turn over and consummation of liquor. On top of the bottles chip technology is installed which measures the exact amount of liquor taken out of the bottles which can then be compared to the drinks sold.

This type of controlling drastically reduced the amount of alcohol that regularly had to be written off before that smart technological move. The controlling works through an app on a tablet PC.

For those of you visiting Las Vegas and who do not want to miss a flavor of the good old days when the city was a bit more on the trashy side, there are still a few establishments in some side roads off the Strip. Those who want to ´warp´ into the days of Bugsy Siegel may want to visit the

---

[21] Source: Adam Tanner: What stays in Vegas

Mob Museum. There you can get your picture taken as a mug shot like on a ´Wanted´ poster.

Regardless what you are looking for. You probably always will find a piece of it in Vegas.

<u>Movie and TV Recommendations:</u>
- *Ocean´s Eleven starring Dean Martin*
- *Ocean`s Eleven starring George Clooney*
- *Vegas starring Robert Urich*

12. Sovereignty on demand

Freedom of the individual in general is a high, not to be underestimated value and in most countries, at least for those under the western hemisphere, freedom is embedded in the respective constitutions in one way or the other.

However, personal freedom in a society does not mean, that people are free to do whatever they like or please. It rather means moving freely within a defined frame to allow everyone to express freedom equally. Problems arise when someone wants to obtain a level of freedom by taken it from someone else.

Some of those who believe they are subject to their own specially defined types of freedom belong to a movement in the United States called ´Sovereign Citizens´. You may already rightfully conclude, that these strange fellow citizens living up to this sub-culture can be rather found in the rural areas and in the suburbs in the Mid and South West than in the melting pots of the big cities.

These fighters for freedom consider themselves as citizens of their home state but not necessarily as citizens of the United States of America. They are referring to certain wording in the U.S. constitution, which seem to confirm their views by simultaneously ignoring those portions of the constitution which do not support it.

The supporters of the movement like to refer to the Declaration of Independence and the Federalist Papers, the series of newspaper articles written by John Jay, Alexander Hamilton and James Madison published from 1787 under the pseudonym Anonymous, which are considered the basis of the transformation of individual states to a union of states[22].

This notion of a rather loose knit of otherwise independent states was widely spread until the break-out of the war between the Blue in the North and the Grey in the South. President Andrew Jackson too is said to have viewed the states more as a union of separate states, much like the European Union today. Somewhere between 100,000 and 200,000 U.S. citizens are considered part of the Sovereign Citizens movement. Exact numbers are difficult to obtain as these people are organized in small bands without club houses. The `Sovereigns`, in general, believe that federal laws and regulations are illegitimate.

The interesting part of it is, that these views typically unearth when the central government in Washington remind its citizens of their obligations, like paying taxes or follow-up on legal actions.

However, once those proud citizens aim for or are in need of benefits from the federal government and its institutions, Medicare, Medicaid or Social Security come to mind, and collecting federal checks, they seem to be pretty glad again to be part of United States. Those self-proclaimed

---

[22] Source: http://thomas.loc.gov/home/histdox/fedpapers.html accessed on February 17, 2015

independent citizens typically find their way into the public spotlight when they have to appear in front of a judge. In such cases they claim that federal laws do not apply to them and they believe not having to pay income tax or parking tickets.

They also like to write threatening letters to judges or officers and even issue warrants to them. It are stories like these that at first sound somewhat amusing if these people would not take their case rather serious and at times end up violently.

Some fellows of the sovereign movement caused international attention early 2016 when they occupied a strip of land in the Malheur Wildlife Refuge in Oregon. It started with some guys sentenced to prison for setting fire on public land occupying public land in Harney County and spreading talk of sparking a movement to overthrow the Government[23]. It ended with a stand-off between the occupiers and the FBI and Oregon State Police and with one occupier dead. The FBI and police found a truckload of semi-automatic rifles and several handguns. The whole incident cost several million Dollars which will mostly have to be covered by the tax payers.

Movie Recommendations:
- *Red Dawn starring Patrick Swayze*
- *Invasion USA starring Chuck Norris*

---

[23] Source: USA Today, January 5, 2016

13. You better be prepared…

Do you belong to the type of people who like to prepare for upcoming events? Have you ever planned and booked your next holiday trip a year in advance? Have you ever bought the first Christmas presents back in May? There is nothing wrong with that!

In the United States there are people who show similar behaviors but go much further in their intent and efforts to preparing for larger, mostly undefined events. Americans who are preparing for the time after the time as we know it are called 'Preppers´, deriving from the word preparation. What are these people preparing for? Who are these visionaries and what are they doing to be prepared for those unforeseeable events?

Specialized books, magazines and websites provide uncountable speculations, mysteries, conspiracies and theories of very bad things that are meant to happen any day now. Riots and plunder in the street by the walking poor or invasions from the outside, whoever that may be, or worse things are just the beginning and from there it is downhill.

McDonalds is running out of burgers and Starbucks is getting short on hot milk to serve lattes to name just a few of those horrible developments that could occur once the end is near. Dramatic events could happen practically overnight and would change the way of life in the land of the Free. So you better be prepared!

The prepper movement started big time in the 1930s[24] during the depression years causing some to fear that the society as a whole is at the brink of its existence. But change was on the way. Once the economy started to grow again and, a few years later, the U.S. entered World War II, the people, for good reasons, had better things to worry about than to prepare for bad, imagined times, get buried in the middle of nowhere or piling up canned food.

The second wave of the prepping sub-culture has arisen during the cold war when many feared a nuclear war between the U.S. and the Soviet Union or that the Bering Street may freeze again causing an imminent invasion of communists. The prepping business kept on hanging in there with its ups and downs way into the 1980s, when the nuclear arms race between the former USSR and the USA reached new highs during the first term of the Reagan administration.

20 years later preppers had another field day in 1999, when the millennia again caused fears of devastation and downturn. Every time such a phase came, the survival business boomed. When the world is coming to an end you need to have a lot of equipment for the day after.

Today, the fears originate from inside the country, which triggers the impulse in some to better be prepared. The prepper movement suspects the president that he wants to take away their weapons and to turn the

---

[24] Source: Wikipedia, Survivalism, accessed on May 12, 2015

country into a socialist enclave where every person is legally entitled to health insurance. O tempores; o mores.

What exactly do those preppers do while preparing for the end of time or worse? What makes them different from ordinary people? Real preppers are a mixture of self-accredited survival specialists, sovereign citizens and people attracted to all kinds of conspiracies, you know, the Kennedy assassination by anyone but Oswald, the fake landing on the Moon and Elvis still roaming through super markets. In essence, it is opposition to anything that has to do with the government.

In total it is a mixed menu, where some simple minded Americans are ignoring any conclusions, opinions and, most importantly, facts that are not closely in line with their own conspirator mindset. This type of mental stew is not for the taste of everyone which keeps the number or preppers at decent numbers.

A safe place for the day when the world as we now it is no more is one of the first things a real prepper must have as a hide-out in case any of his conspiracy theories come true. An unfriendly take-over by the federal government or attacks by foreign forces are typical conspiracy theories of preppers. Don´t ask which foreign countries that might be as long as the United States spends more on the military than almost all other nations on this planed combined. But then, what do we know?

Some believe an attack, from the inside or the outside, may start with a country-wide electromagnetic impulse. After that, so the conspiracy goes, there will be no more power anywhere and the land of the free is thrown back to the Stone Age practically overnight and you need to be prepared for that.

Anyway, there is nothing that would stop a thorough-bred prepper from owning and maintaining a secure spot somewhere. For the worst of all times the minimum requirement is a bunker. Compared to Europe, there are almost no bunkers left from times of war in America. Moving to Europe, where there are still thousands of bunkers left from WW II, is unthinkable for most Americans, especially for preppers. So, what to do?

Quite easy; if there is no bunker, you just build one. Preppers like to have their bunkers built somewhere in the wilderness but, of course, only as far out as the sacred place can be reached comfortably in a short period of time by SUV.

Those bunkers are typically equipped with everything what someone might need for the time after the time. A well for fresh water, generators, plenty of food, durable for decades and, not to forget, guns, the more the better, are all on top the preparation list.

Some of the preppers spend quite some of their leisure time in their bunkers. You probably have already guessed that preppers in general and bunker owners in particular are almost exclusively men, white men to be precise. However, the wives and children cannot always escape the week-end plans of their patriotic heads of the family.

So they may have to endure long drives into the wide open spaces far from the outskirts of their cozy homes in some suburb and instead of spending the weekend on the golf course or barbequing in the back yard, canned survival food is served in the bunker. The survival food probably lasts an eternity and might have been processed before the war. Let us safe the question which war that might be. The good night´s rest happens deep down in the earth, although you can expect more comfort than in a World War II bunker on the eastern front.

Sometimes there are reports in newspapers or in a TV show covering stories about such bunkers. If a lucky journalist is able to visit any of those bunkers, they are being blindfolded on the trip to the hide-out. They also might have to hand in their cell and smart phones. You never know. Any safety measure is being applied to prevent that bunkers could be detected by an outsider.

Movie Recommendations:
- *Seven Days in May starring Kirk Douglas*
- *Fail Safe starring Henry Fonda*

Part II

Rich and Poor

14. Taxes are for the Poor

Towards the end of the 1920s the richest 1% of the United States reached a new height in financial wealth and had managed to accumulate almost 20% of the national income and to pay almost no taxes on it. Then came the Black Friday and with it the Great Depression followed by a tax reform which considerably increased the income tax rates.

The tax reform introduced a new top tax rate of 94% which only applied to very high income. In fact, this extremely high tax rate was only invented for one single person who also was the only person that would generate income levels that would justify such a tax rate. This particular high income roller was John D. Rockefeller. In general, the new tax rates are considered as one of the main reasons that income and wealth were distributed broader and equally for decades to come.

The top tax rate of more than 90% was maintained at its heights from the 1940s way into the 1960s. A tax rate of 90% or more sounds a lot but of course it needs to be considered that the top rate only set in from a certain income level onwards. Back in 1940 only tax payers with income above USD 200,000 qualified for the 90% tax bracket. Today, that would translate into USD 1,700,000.00.

The results of low unemployment, high work force participation, and high taxes resonating in high income equalization were the main ingredients of the economic boom after World War II. Income excesses were kept at bay and the tax revenues were increased constantly. Among other things, the government invested the tax money in infrastructure projects, particularly the Highway Bill, which financed the current net of Highways and Freeways. Prior to the Highway Bill the United States did not have an interstate highway system. In Germany, Dwight D. Eisenhower saw the Autobahn system and the advantages such a system could have in military logistics. The highway system was meant to provide mobility for the U.S. armed forces as well as for business and civil transportation.

Another reinvestment of tax revenues to the general public was the G.I. Bill. The thousands of homecoming G.I. from Europe and the Pacific needed two things besides reuniting with their families and living a normal life again. They needed education and regular jobs after years of fighting for the country. When they joined the armed forces, some of the soldiers left their old jobs which often were no longer available, whereas others joined up with Uncle Sam right out of school. The G.I. Bill was the starting point of a full swing economic and employment boom.

The income equalization and wide spread distribution of wealth reached vast parts of the population building the foundation of a well situated middle class. During that time the top tax rate was slowly decreased every couple of years to reach about 60% in the 1980s.

In the White House, the former peanut farmer Jimmy Carter was followed by the former actor Ronald Reagan. Ronald Reagan morphed from a rather centered political person in the 1950s into a conservative governor of California and later on into a fiscal hawk and capitalist President during his first term before sliding back to more centered positions in his second term.

Today's conservatives who use Ronald Reagan as their role model for never ending tax cuts, particularly for those already well off, usually embrace his fiscal stance during his first Presidency while ignoring the revenue adjustments he made during his last years in office, mainly a dozen tax increases.

The Reagan administration reduced the already heavily cut top tax rate to under 40%. Added to that were large scale write-off opportunities, massive business subsidies and a reform of the capital gains tax which made making big bucks lucrative again. Those making top dollars could keep an ever larger piece of their gross income.

Today, the top 1% of the population is receiving almost 25% of the total gross income in America which comes with an average tax rate of less than 10% after all possibilities, legal tricks and loopholes are put at work to a maximum.

While the top tax rate was hovering towards 30% during the Presidency of George W. Bush caused by the tax reform of his administration, it has reached 39.6% right now just shy of 40% after the Bush tax cuts expired, which, again, does not mean that many top income receivers really pay top tax rates or any taxes at all as long as the tax code offers plenty of opportunities circumventing it.

The IRS, indirectly also protects the rich from paying too much of a fair share to society. Chronically underfunded and understaffed, some say on purpose, the IRS barely has the resources auditing a decent rate of tax returns. Although the tax code gets more complex every year the IRS audit rate fell to 0.84%, the lowest in a decade.

It means that more than 99 out of 100 tax returns are being processed unaudited. It also means that merely USD 7.32 billion[25] in taxes were collected in 2015 from audits, compared to USD 14.7 billion just 10 years earlier. Outdated technology adds to the problem that tax returns pass the systems unchecked. IRS Commissioner John A. Koskinen said 'we have many applications that were running when John F. Kennedy was President'.

Movie and TV Recommendations:
- *Rich Man, Poor Man starring Peter Strauss*
- *Wall Street starring Michael Douglas*

---

[25] Source: USA Today

15.   One that hath shall be given

In Europe, particularly in Germany, there are ongoing discussions in the media and the public about the feared and perceived rift between the rich and the poor, wherever the definition of either category starts and ends.

The United States has turned itself into a country divided between the haves and the have-nots. There is not much talk in America about the huge gap between the two poles, although it is so obvious wherever you look.

Where there is no much talk, there is no much questioning either, why things are as they are and what lead to it. There is barely any real political debate, media coverage or public uproar. Why is that? Maybe it has to do how the distribution of wealth is perceived by the general public.

Surveys among the general public reveal that the perceived allocation and distribution of income and wealth is almost the same in Germany and the United States. In both countries the people surveyed see a high share of income and wealth at the top of the society, average figures in the so called middle class, or what is left of it, and a small percentage in the lower ranks of the population. Where those two countries differ immensely is the real allocation of income and wealth.

In Germany the actual distribution of wealth is much broader and thus fairer than the people believe. The middle class in particular is far bigger as the perception would tell, while the share of the population of those considered poor is much lower as assumed.

In America it is exactly the other way around. The middle class, once the heart and soul of the American success story during the 20th century, is drifting downwards constantly while the number of low income and poor people goes up almost at the same pace. Many Americans who are already considered poor still believe or consider themselves in the middle class.

As it affects so many someone might not realize how much the middle class deteriorated, as long as neighbors and colleagues are pretty much in the same situation and if there is a short memory how different, and better, it once might have been.

On the tip of the pyramid, where the top 1% or the population hovers around, times were rarely any better than today. Looking at a larger percentage, the top 10% of the population, we see that about 80% of the income goes to roughly 30 million people. That is a lot of money going to a lot of people which explains in part why the United States are still doing pretty good economically although 270 million people sharing the remaining, merely 20% of the distributable income.

The 1970s was the decade where the income distribution reached a level that could be best described as fair. During those colorful years only

8% of the income went to the top 1% whereas today´s high percentage of 25% was last seen in the 1930s before the high tax rates set in[26].

<u>Movie Recommendations</u>
- *Margin Call starring Demi Moore*
- *The Big Short starring Christian Bale*

---

[26] Source: Thomas Piketty & Emmanuel Saez (2007); Capital 11/2014

16. Can you feel the wealth?

I f people are being asked about income distribution based on real amounts and median calculation, surveys show an equally controversial picture between the United States and Germany.

Those surveys were looking at the share of the population making 60% of the median, those who were exactly on the median and those considered at the upper end of the scale at 250% in relation to the median.

The median is the calculated middle-value, not to be mixed-up or mistaken with the average value. A usual method to calculate the median is to take the highest figure and lowest, adding them together and dividing them by two. Let us use an example to illustrate it.

Let us take a monthly income of USD 2,000 as being the median. Now we are asking the population to assess, estimate or bluntly guess what percentage of the population makes USD 1,200 or 60% of the median and how many make USD 5,000 or 250% of the median.

Interestingly, people surveyed in America and Germany equally believe that about 22% of the population receives a monthly income of USD 1,200. In reality the picture looks a bit different. In Germany, the percentage of people earning USD 1,200 a month is approximately 15% and lower than perceived. On the other side of the Atlantic 30% of the population are in this lower category thus way higher than people think. The first conclusion is that Germans seem to believe that way more people are low income receivers than it is the case and that the opposite applies to Americans.

The top of the income scale provides similar controversies. In Germany as well as in the United States of America people surveyed believe that 7.5% of the population makes USD 5,000 a month. Real figures provide that the percentage in Germany is closer to 2.5%, while in the United States the opinion matches the facts, itself a very rare case where perceptions and real numbers are practically the same.

Germans seem to believe that way more of their fellow residents would belong to the upper income brackets while the Americans seem to be pretty accurate in concluding the percentage of recipients of income in the USD 5,000 bracket.

Why are the assumptions or estimations about income distribution in most cases in stark contrast to the real numbers? Why does Germany assume that incomes on top and the bottom are drifting away from the median, when in fact incomes are rather close to the median? Why, on the other hand, do the Americans believe that there is a strong income concentration close to the median and considerably underestimates the large part of the population in the low income section?

One important source leading to this kind of divergence could be the media and the way these report on income and wealth distribution on either side of the Atlantic. Depending on the focus of media reporting opinions about the subject seem to shift in one or the other direction.

In the German tabloids and in certain TV shows reports on poverty of the elderly and precarious incomes are a regular part of the media coverage what could lead to the conclusion that the portion of poor people as a percentage of the population would be considerably higher than in reality.

In the United States, the media, particularly the hundreds of TV stations provide a rather optimistic picture of the income situation of the American people. Even if incomes are low and many can barely make ends meet, times are not as bad as they may appear and, as always, the best is yet to come. The lousy job, or two or three of them to get around will not last long and the top and well paid jobs may just lurk around the next corner.

Add to that the old belief that after an economic downturn a successful rebound is inevitable. At least that much was true for some parts of the recent past during the 20th century. But obviously this economic phenomena did not work out so well this time around as far as low income families and the middle class are affected. Incomes in the lower ranks dropped drastically after the 2008 meltdown or ´The Great Recession´, in memory of ´The Great Depression´ and barely recovered since then [27]

Movie Recommendations:
- *The richest girl in the world starring Joel McCrea*

---

[27] Source: Thomas Piketty & Emmanuel Saez (2007) and Capital 11/2014, page 89

Part III

The Circus of Politics

17. The never-ending Election

T here is the saying 'After the election is before the election'. Since many years this applies to America more than it probably does to any other country on this beautiful planet.

If you grab the remote and flip through the numerous news channels on your TV and let us also assume you manage to stay with one channel for more than just a few minutes to watch the insanity that is playing out in front of you, you really may get the impression that the next election is due the very next day even if the previous election night happened to be yesterday.

The counting of the votes – do you remember the Bush-Gore fiasco? – of the previous election is barely over and the elected representatives of the people have taken their new posts, the media machine seems to get in full gears towards the next election. Most of the attention is naturally given to the Presidential election, particularly the upcoming, inevitable line-up of soon to be candidates in the next primaries.

This sometimes quite entertaining first roll call of Presidential hopefuls is the first chapter towards the caucuses and primaries. At this stage of the election cycle, which seems to start even earlier every time around, it does not even matter if a person already declared whether he or she is really running for office or is purely ´exploring the options´, short for looking whether there are enough cash donors to fill the coffers required for a successful campaign.

If we take a look who finally gets elected and how little a U.S. President is able to achieve with a divided Congress, cost and benefit for a temporary stay of four or eight years in the White House are completely out of line. Some say that the 2016 presidential election will probably cost north of USD 4 billion. The show that is put on for the voters is either worth every penny of it or it is throwing money out of the window, depending on the point of view.

I am following the U.S. presidential and congressional elections for at least 20 years now, especially in the waning weeks of summer when the campaigns are in full swing towards the elections in November.

In that phase the TV stations are on election mode 24/7 and it appears as if there is no air time left that is not filled with political reports, debates and commercials, paid by the parties, donors and the so called Super PACs. If you really want to escape the election circus you literally have to get lost somewhere in the wilderness.

But even to get out there by driving on some hidden highway, you may have to endure an army of plastered roadside signs and the cars in front of you carry bumper stickers for or against a party or a candidate.

I particularly remember a bumper sticker back from 2004. It happened on a drive through Montana somewhere between Butte and Missoula, when a car up front carried a bumper sticker showing the faces of President Bush, Cheney and Rumsfeld and the line ´The Asses of Evil´, hitting on the ´Axis of Evil´ slander which started the quagmire in Iraq and ended with the ill-rotten support given to the various rebel groups during the so-called Arab Spring, triggered the civil war in Syria and the unrest in Iraq, Yemen, Libya and Egypt, the rise of ISIS as a new terrorist force, the assaults in Paris as well as the fugitive crisis in Europe. ´Another fine mess you put us in to´ as Oliver Hardy used to say when Stan Laurel caused them some trouble again.

Movie Recommendations:
- *City Hall starring John Cusack*
- *House of Cards starring Kevin Spacey*
- *Hello Mr. President starring Michael Douglas*
- *Dave starring Kevin Kline*
- *Tit for that starring Stan Laurel and Oliver Hardy*

18. Two parties – No choice

In the United States it comes down to a political system consisting of only two parties. Apart from that, attempts to establish other parties or having a candidate running as an independent providing at least a third option for the people rarely surface, thinking of Ross Perot or Ralph Nader. At least for the Presidential election, very few exceptions aside, a Democratic and a Republican candidate are facing each other in the end.

Today, the two-party system leaves little room for fresh ideas and building common ground, particularly on federal level, as long as these two parties are as deeply polarized as the Democrats and Republicans. Common sense and the best interest for the people have no chance today to prevail in such a dire situation.

The foundation for this system was already built at the very early days of the United States. During the establishment of the Union there where the Republicans, not related to the Republicans today, which were headed by Thomas Jefferson on the one side and the Federalists on the other.

The Republicans wanted the Unites States to be a loose collaboration of otherwise independent states, more in the sense of the European Union today, whereas the Federalists - nomen est omen - favored the federal union pretty much the way it exists today.

In the middle of the 19th century there were the Democrats and the Whigs and later, at the times of Abraham Lincoln, the Democrats and Republicans where the two leading parties. The positions and focus of those two parties shifted considerably throughout time.

During the Abraham Lincoln Administration the Democrats dominated the South destined to stay that way for the next 100 years. Democrats back then were considered conservative, rurally rooted, maintaining traditions and not too keen on progress, very much the way Republicans consider themselves these days.

Republicans back then on the other hand were known for rather 'leftish', liberal and democratic tendencies. The most famous Republican President was Abraham Lincoln, who campaigned for the abolishment of the slavery in the U.S. This intent alone was enough for the 'right' and conservative Democrats from the South to secede from the Union and to establish the Confederate States of America under President Jefferson Davis.

Then like now the political system in Washington had little understanding for the cause and interest of the rural population. Back then, similar to today's issue of handling issues like illegal immigration, it were the different views and opinions for and against slaves, who made up to

50% of the population of some of the states in the South of about 12 million at the advent of the Civil War. [28]

The Republicans of the Presidency of Abraham Lincoln were regionally popular in the Northeast and their supporters could be found among entrepreneurs and people keen on technological progress. The slavery question was by far the most dividing issue between the two parties.

The Democrats were strong supporters; the Republicans equally strongly opposed keeping other humans as slaves. The result is history. After 5 years of bloody Civil War and more than 500,000 deaths, counting those who died of hunger and diseases that number is estimated up to a million, the slavery question was answered once for all.

Movie Recommendations:
- *Shenandoah starring James Stewart*
- *Lincoln starring Daniel Day-Lewis*

---

[28] Source: The Political Crisis of the 1850s – Michael F. Holt, W.W. Norton Company, 1978

19. Slaves balancing the votes

From the early days of the United State of America strong differences in the population numbers existed between the northern and southern founding states.

This would have caused a strong imbalance on the number of representatives a state could send to the House of Representatives, which, then as now, was based on the population of a state eligible to vote. In that regard, the southern population felt strongly disadvantaged. But help was on the way.

Where there was a lack of white men eligible to vote, there were plenty of black slaves. The black men had no right to vote, well, basically they had no rights at all to start with, but this was no reason to have their numbers count as part of the population.

Women, regardless which skin color, could not vote either and were not equipped with the same rights given to their male counterparts. Back then too, the ´land of the free´ meant different things to different people and left plenty of room for interpretation.

The southern states were granted to count their slaves at $2/3^{rds}$ to the population count, increasing the number of representatives the southern states could send to the House. It is no surprise that this distasteful and inhumane ruling caused heated debates among the political leaders of the young nation before it was approved, considering that slavery was already viewed very critical in the northern states and frequent calls for abolishment of keeping humans as slaves were common.

Movie Recommendations:
- *Django Unchained starring Jamie Foxx*
- *Duel at Diablo starring James Garner*
- *Skin Game starring James Garner*

20.   Tell me where you live...

Who wants to figure out, which party is most likely going to win in a particular precinct does not necessarily have to wait till the votes are counted on election night.

It seems to have become a core task of the elected officials, regardless which party, to draw and redraw the precincts. What is the purpose behind this creative drawing of lines on the landscape? It is not hard to conclude.

After each election both parties are analyzing how the votes turned out in each single district to ensure that the results will be more predictable, thus ´right´ the next time around.

As this is artfully done by both parties, it is quite obvious where this is leading after a while. After each election cycle the political strategists from either party find it increasingly easier predicting the result of an election by purely applying arithmetic.

This principle equally works in a city as it does on state level. Added to that is the fact that certain cities, regions and states by strong majority tend toward one or the other party, leaving little room for exceptions and miscalculations.

States like California or New York are firmly in Democratic hands whereas Texas or Wyoming dominantly votes Republican. This oddity came to play again at election night 2012.

Once the majority of battle ground states clearly moved towards President Barack Obama, he was named the winner against Mitt Romney. Karl Rove, the mastermind behind the ´shock and awe´ fear campaign of 2004, was sitting in a Fox News studio with Megyn Kelly when she and Fox News declared Barrack Obama the winner and Karl got bananas over it, wanting to wait till all the votes are counted. It obviously was hard for him losing out to a system he catered and nurtured for so long without realizing that one day it may turn against him.

It could be suggested, at least for Presidential elections, that people do not even have to go to the ballots in states where the results are already clear before the votes are in. This way the election apparatus of the two parties as well as the media could focus all their energy on the battle ground states, keeping up the tension in an election cycle. But we are in a 24/7 news world where dozens of news stations are competing for something big to fill the ´breaking news´ tag line.

The drawing of the precincts by party lines even helps when looking for a new home or an apartment. It is no secret that Americans in general like to live among equals, people that look much like themselves, share similar beliefs and values as well as showing comparable levels of wealth, education and employment.

Those who want to know it all just need to visit some of those specific websites, where you can get all the information on a town, a region or a precinct. You can find out about the age structure of the population, the ethnic diversity and the religious affiliations. This prevents that someone may accidentally gets ´lost´ in the wrong part of town.

As Democrats and Republicans can be assured of ever more precincts that they are safely going to win or surely loose, regardless what the candidates propagate, it leaves them plenty of opportunities to focus on those parts of the country were results cannot easily be predicted and undecided souls need convincing, and plenty of convincing it is.

Among others, it requires hopeful candidates to leave previous positions or common sense behind by proposing something big, like building a wall – a nice wall – along the Mexican border or rounding-up and deporting 11 million illegal immigrants. Who wants to get elected, has to aim for the stars or at least promise them.

Movie Recommendations:
- *Election starring Reese Witherspoon*
- *Something Big starring Dean Martin*

21.   Battle for ideologies

Since the 2012 election cycle the Republicans seem to have had only one goal for which they worked themselves off. Getting rid of Obamacare seemed to be the only thing that mattered to a Party that occupied both, the House and the Senate. By mid 2015 more than 60(!) legislative and judicative attempts are on record to block or repeal the law for general health insurance in Congress and on any which way towards implementation.

Some might think opposing just one law would be enough justification for getting elected. It is quite surprising what little voters expect from their elected officials nowadays. Four years earlier the House got off with an equally bad start when the Republican majority leader outlined the goal for the Republican House representatives during the first presidency of Barack Obama. He declared that the main task would be to ensure that Barack Obama would be a one-term president. This goal too, similar to Obamacare later on, failed though.

I still struggle to understand how deep the hate for the political opposition must be to waste all this energy fighting an uphill battle to the end. Just because an initiative like health care, where America spends more than four times the average of other Western countries but still has a lower life expectancy then the others, was brought to the table by the opposing party. The Republicans literally gridlocked Congress instead of proposing own initiatives and alternatives where common ground would be possible. But compromises seem to be bad for the record if someone wants to be President someday.

There is an interesting twist to the Affordable Care Act. While some Republican Representatives and Senators are still on the ´Repeal Obamacare´ track, the Governors in their home states have taken the pragmatic road. Governors from states like Arizona, Nevada, New Mexico or South Dakota have expanded Medicaid under the Affordable Care Act[29].

The on-set of the 2016 presidential campaign almost provided for another battle ground. This time around it could have been the education initiative Common Core. The goal of Common Core is to define and to develop federally comparable testing standards for High Schools and Colleges without questioning or challenging the competence of the states regarding topics and content. A pretty good idea some would say, ensuring that a High School diploma from South Dakota is comparable to the same degree in New York.

This initiative passed the U.S. Congress with a great majority, particularly supported by many votes from the Republicans. But, and from here on it gets difficult, the Common Core is an initiative driven forward by

---

[29] Source: New York Times, December 28, 2015

President Obama, so the Republicans, naturally, have to strongly oppose it, even if they strongly supported it in the first place.

But when an election is coming up, some candidates don't want to be caught in bed with the enemy's ideas, regardless how good they are. The Republicans even found another fancy name for the initiative; Obamacore, which further helped bedeviling it.

But it did not get very far. The Common Core was barely covered in any of the Republican debates. Unfortunately, these dramatized shows have no resemblance with the traditional meaning of a debate. It turned out that the show provided by Trump, Cruz & Co. left no space to discuss this or any other issue in some depth and detail allowing the electorate building an opinion.

Movie and TV Recommendations:
- *The Best Man starring Henry Fonda*
- *Veep starring Julia Louis-Dreyfus*

22. Who needs clean hands anyway?

I it is a popular move to use the individual freedom of the population for political proliferation. In this aspect, some Republicans use the fight for freedom, real or just imagined, to fight the opposing candidate, mostly a Democrat, in a political race on state or federal level, particularly if a TV camera is nearby.

What some initiatives focusing on the protection of the freedom of the individual have in common is that the influence the federal Government in Washington has upon the states and communities should be fenced in and reduced to a minimum.

Of course it is not the intent of the protectors of freedom to turn the voters into revolutionaries taking it up with Uncle Sam. It is just a nice stunt against the political contender and also helps to fill the daily schedule of news programming.

A nice example for this type of political play is a decade old federal regulations. In restaurants where guests and staff jointly use the same restrooms there has to be sign applicable for the waiters, cooks, bus buys and anyone else working in the eatery, to wash their hands in the bathroom before returning to work.

Let us forget for a moment that washing hands after going to the bathroom should be natural thing, regardless whether you are visiting a restaurant or if you are working there. It should not require a sign at all and I cannot remember any country where staff needs reminding.

But this is America and I have long ago stopped questioning some of the strange proceedings and regulations you are stumbling upon every now and then and where nobody else in the country seems to be wondering about it why such a sign is needed in the first place. There is the even stranger question, how someone could get the idea using a bathroom sign that most don´t even notice anymore as a tool in the fight against the federal Government. But let us start from the beginning.

Senator Thom Tillis from North Carolina, you might have guessed it already, a Republican, was aiming for his 15 Minutes of TV[30] fame by suggesting that restaurant owners should no longer be forced requiring their employees to wash their hands after a trip to the bath room. It should be voluntary for a waiter or a cook to return to work with clean hands.

Let us ignore for a moment what impact this would have on the guests of a restaurant once they get the news that washing hands for staff is optional. It can be assumed that even in the land of the free, freedom has its limits. Fans of the TV sitcom ´Seinfeld´ may remember the episode where Jerry Seinfeld is just washing his hands in a restroom when the restaurant

---

[30] Source Ile: BBC News

owner and chef comes out of the stall and went straight back to work getting his hands on to some dough of pizza. The look on Jerry`s face said it all and we probably can imagine how we would feel in such a case.

The argument of the simple minded Senator is, that it can´t be that law abiding restaurant owners and their fellow burger flippers are being told by some Washington bureaucrats if and to what extent hygienic seems appropriate.

To keep guests informed, or scared away, he offered an alternative that owners of eateries could put up a sign, that washing hands for employees is voluntary in their establishment. One sign would thus be replaced by another and one regulation replaced by another. But maybe this conclusion did not cross the Senator´s mind.

Movie and TV Recommendations:
- *The Bird Cage starring Robin Williams*
- *Seinfeld starring Jerry Seinfeld*

23. The Winner takes it all

Y ou may well remember the drama of the election year 2000 when the Presidential race was so close that counting a few hundred votes turned out to be difficult and the recounting looked like an act from the stone age, straight out of a 'The Flintstones' episode. Watching officials on TV looking at voting cards and whether there were any holes in there was a mixture between a thriller and right out slapstick.

In the end of this drama, that did not seem to come to an end, it was left to the courts to determine, if Bush or Gore should be declared the winner and become President. Every banana republic seemed to be more advanced in that moment.

Four years later the next election came up and with it a new script by the strategists how to be win the election. The Republicans quite obvious had the better script writers headed by Karl Rove and his tactical campaign of 'Fear and Terror'. No rally, no speech, no posters and no TV ad without scary pictures and the message that the country would be the victim of terror and other bad things without Bush, war and torture.

The highly decorated Vietnam veteran John Kerry, the secretary of state during the second Obama term, had no chance against George W.

Bush and Dick Cheney, who both smartly dodged the bullet being drafted for Vietnam duty.

The smear campaign resulted in Kerry being discredit as too weak as Commander in Chief and, if elected, would weaken America and playing right into the hands the enemy. Remember ´Swift Boat Veterans for Truth´?

Movie and TV Recommendations:
- *The Flintstones (Animated)*

24.   Hot air from Alaska

The election year 2008, as far as I was able to judge, was the first year of a Presidential election in which content, a program, a vision or whatever some might expect from a civilized election played a supporting role at best.

It was a kind of a political soap opera with some surreal episodes. It started with some TV commercials and ads which only seem to be possible in America.

The campaigns of either party raise millions in donations and further millions collected by the Super PACs to place ads on TV no longer presenting their candidate as the brave knight on the white horse that would bring heaven on earth if elected.

The ads of today's election only seem to have one purpose; to discredit or frankly demonize the opposing candidate on the other side of the aisle.

We are probably already numb by the bombardments of ads that circulating in the tube and online day and night close to the election. Among the types of ads there is one type of negative ads which are more disgusting than others.

Those usually start by depicting a statement from an opposing candidate, which, completely taken out of context, is then dramatized like in a reality show. It does not matter when the statement was made, verbally in Congress or on TV, in writing in a book, an op-ed in a newspaper or an article for the High School magazine.

Whatever it was that the candidate did or may have said is twisted until the original message is no longer recognizable. In the ad, the message is then presented that the world as we now it will be no more if the opposing candidate would be elected.

On the Democratic side it was Hillary Clinton heavily battling the then almost unknown Senator Barack Obama with a truck load of hard hitting ads to no avail, as history can tell.

The Republicans sent John McCain into the race. Like his friend, the aforementioned John Kerry, John McCain was a former Vietnam veteran whom I considered a tough and conservative but yet moderate Republican Senator.

Due to his own horrible experience in Vietnam while captive as prisoner of war, he was an outspoken sceptic, if not critic of the so-called ´enhanced interrogation methods´ as torture is being called in conservative circles and in the media to make it sound less inhumane and more acceptable by the American public.

He was tortured while being a prisoner and thus had plenty reasons to distance himself from those 'techniques'. He was also an outspoken sceptic of the way the wars in Iraq and Afghanistan were handled.

His advisers must have gotten the idea that, to win over the conservative base as well as undecided voters, their candidate had to be presented as much tougher, take-no-prisoners type of hard core conservative. Positioned like this, he would pose as a real alternative compared to the perceived weak candidate the Democratic side had sent into the Presidential race.

But then he or at least some of his advisers must have completely lost their minds. As John McCain really did not have the looks of a poster boy following in the footsteps or, even better, the hoofs of the All-American Cowboy, Ronald Reagan, they started searching for a running mate who at least looked good on TV.

They seemed to have hit the jackpot when they picked the then Governor of Alaska, Sarah Palin. Coming from the Nordic province, dressed in haute couture, equipped with designer glasses that made her at least look somewhat intelligently she was pushed into the spotlight literally overnight.

What she was standing for politically or if she brought any experience to the table that could be expected from someone who may take the reins of number two in the White House seemed completely irrelevant. At first the main focus was to show her around making sure she would get as much national attention as possible. However, there were moments where she had to say something, even without a teleprompter at hand.

Whenever she appeared in public and had to speak freely, she just let it out what she had on her mind, which wasn't much. Some of her scary statements made many realize that she seemed to have no qualifications at all required for the Vice Presidency and made people wonder how it would be in a real case, where she would have to steer the fate of the world with her hands on the 'Football', the nuclear codes.

After he lost the election and to this very day, he was and still is a Senator from Arizona but retained his new conservative state of mind taken on during the 2008 campaign. His moderate days seem to be gone. Whenever we hear from him on international policy it sounds as he would be ready to go to war against the bad guys out there, be it Syria or maybe even playing with fire against Russia.

Sarah Palin remained on high demand in the media circles as constant guest and commentator on Fox News and book author. Today she still appears on TV occasionally and is well connected with the remainders of the once popular Tea Party fraction.

She also still appears regularly in the tabloids, particularly when her daughter has another child out of wedlock or her son gets arrested in stark contrast to the conservative views and family values she propagated.

However, parodying her, like Tina Fey did so prominently, has gone somewhat out of fashion.

Early 2016 she made a brief ´comeback´ when she endorsed Donald Trump for President. Gladly, it was only a brief moment.

<u>Movie Recommendations:</u>
- *North to Alaska starring mit John Wayne*
- *Death Hunt starring Charles Bronson*

25. America got talent

I n the election cycle 2012 the re-election campaign of Barack Obama was the center of the attention. There were no Democratic candidates challenging him so it was an all-out battle between the Republican candidates and the incumbent President.

As there was no Democratic primary which would have provided some entertainment, all the fun had to come from the Republican side. The Republican primaries far exceeded any expectations. The three ring circus which comes to town every four years rarely offered a better show. The debates could have easily competed for a comedy price if they were a sitcom or a slapstick show.

Most of the Republican contenders of the year 2012 are already forgotten today and many went back home, wherever that was.

Some of them surfaced again during the 2016 Republican primaries but more on that later on. Let us first focus on 2012 and the roster of yesteryears hopefuls. The candidates back then used all their energy to fight the guy currently occupying the White house, who some of them still considered a foreign-born, socialist, Muslim.

Besides the general dislike of President Obama as a person, it was his signature health insurance which was the main issue uniting the Republicans. It could had been anything, but general health care covered by a federal system, standard in literally all developed and even most developing countries, appeared to be the perfect initiative in the crusade for the Presidency. But as it so happened, to no avail. You can't always win as history is repeatedly teaching us.

To win the primaries and to qualify for the political Superbowl against the incumbent, the hopefuls first had to survive the casting shows on TV also known as the Presidential debates. As there can only be one to win it all in the end, the candidates had to 'hold-no-barrels' during the heated discussions on prime time TV. Take the immigration debate as an example, which became a hot issue again four years later.

Republican candidates who merely indicated paving a way for the 11 or 12 million illegal immigrants into legal status were verbally nailed to the wall by the others who in return offered their proposals, ranging from the preposterous to the impossible, how to protect the border from future immigration attempts from Mexico as well as deporting those already illegally in the country.

One planned to complete the already existing fence along the whole border from east to west. The next wanted to extend the fence by doubling up the height and another thought of frying illegals by electrifying the fence. The candidates were equally enthusiastic in deporting those already in the country illegally. However, back then like today none could offer a reasonable way accomplishing the task of ´rounding-up´ 11 or 12 million people and transporting them back to…well, where exactly? Mexico, Guatemala, San Salvador, or elsewhere?

To their excuse it must be said; nobody really asked for such level of detail. There would be no easy way even in the best of intentions. The United States does not have a public register and does not issue identity cards, neither on federal nor on state level.

So it is quite tricky finding out where someone lives and, even more important, whether someone is in the country legally or illegally. For identification or evidence of residence a driver's license, a public library pass or even a heating bill seems to be sufficient. This is the pragmatic and contemporary way things are sometimes done by the leader of the free world, even in the 21st century.

Even after those millions of illegals would be identified somehow, the next logistic challenges would arise. How to ship those people to and across the border? The idea of busses came up. Imagine that; putting 11 million people, who might have lived in America for decades, worked their part for the economy to grow, started their families and sent their kids to school, who then went on joining the workforce themselves and paid tax, into hundreds of busses, crossing the borders into Mexico and other countries back and forth for a couple of years.

A few candidates of the election year 2012 and some of their actions deserve being remembered. One of the first to volunteer for the chair in the White House was Mitt Romney, who was Governor of Massachusetts and organizer of the Olympic winter games in Salt Lake City before he became the Republican candidate.

In his governing role he proudly signed into law a social health care system for the good of all people in the state. When he started his campaign he first took a 180 degree and all of a sudden was against the federal health care system sponsored by President Obama although many features of the law were merely carbon copies of the Massachusetts law.

This earned him a welcome to the club of flip-floppers as a person who today says one thing and does the opposite tomorrow. Supporters of a flip-flopper might claim that it is just a sign of high flexibility if someone changes his mind, even daily if required.

The second big previous job was being a successful project manager of the Olympic winter games which he never stopped mentioning when asked for his qualifications to be President.

During the final stages of the preparations for the Olympic summer games 2012 in London Mitt Romney could not help it, diagnosing from the distance the state of organization in the United Kingdom. He stipulated that London would have done a bad job and would not be ready for the opening of the games. Prime Minister Cameron heard the criticism from overseas and responded laconically that not everything might already be perfectly organized but then it is always easier to organize Olympic Games in the middle of nowhere.

After he lost the election big time he somehow disappeared from the public surface, meaning he was not seen on TV much. He re-surfaced for a brief but shocking moment early 2015 when he, contrary to earlier promises, raised eyebrows by saying he would considering running again. But this moment was so brief, hardly anyone probably remembers it. Little has been heard of him until recently when he made a statement against Donald Trump. Some commentators called it a campaign speech and speculated whether he considers himself as the 'fallback' option.

Then there was Michelle Bachmann, another bright light from the outer far right, who came, was seen and lost, just like Sarah Palin. Political experience seemed to be non-existence despite her short intermezzo as Representative of the House in her home state.

She balanced this deficit by strong religious views and conservative, somewhat outrageous statements. She said simple things but could scare the hell out of you which earned her a title on Time Magazine which scared us even more. At the height of her stardom she won the so-called Straw Poll, the first unofficial poll in the primaries.

But as it so happens with any moments; they are gone the next moment. In another life she might had been a nurse or even a doctor. Her medical skills came to play when she provided some diagnosis from the distance by insinuating that certain vaccinations to students should be abolished because of the side effects. No idea, where she read that or who whispered it into her ears but it provided fodder for the news shows.

Later on she suggested it was the wrath of god when people died in a storm. That must had been too much even for hardcore conservatives and she was gone after the primaries had barely started. Since then, even less was heard from her than from the already very quiet good ole Mitt.

A bit further in the religious corner there were Rick Santorum, who won Iowa, and Mike Huckabee, the Iowa winner of 2008, who covered any shortage of political programs with denunciation of the evolution and classified climate change as a questionable theory at best.

Mike Huckabee even was a Governor, proofing once more that, for some states at least, it does not seem to take any qualification or experience. After he dropped out of the primaries he became a commentator and show master on Fox News, what else, and earned an even better living by selling books to his flock.

The last candidate who comes to mind, there were some more, was Rick Perry, the former Governor of Texas who will forever be remembered for not remembering which were the three federal agencies he wanted to close. Oops.

Santorum, Huckabee and Perry were the three of the Republican class of 2012 who gave it another try four years later.

. Movie Recommendations:
- *Morning Glory starring Harrison Ford*
- *The President's Analyst starring James Coburn*
- *Three-Ring-Circus starring Dean Martin*

26.   The Trump Card

I n some way the Presidential campaigns of 2008, 2012 and 2016 seem to be reboots of the same script. Again, there are very few Democratic candidates, only 3 made it to the debates in 2015, providing not much entertainment. After the primary in New Hampshire there were only Hillary Clinton and Bernie Sanders.

On the other side of the aisle the Republican candidates did their very best to lower the standards even further. Who thought that the Republican roster of unqualified candidates of 2012 could hardly be worse was proven ill wrong when the 2016 list of candidates surfaced in the course of 2015.

After so many years of bad showings the question may be allowed why it has become so difficult for the Republican Party nowadays identifying and selecting candidates who at least could somewhat be considered qualified moving into the White House.

This reminds me of a book, the comedian Jim Hightower once wrote where the title said it all; 'If the gods had meant us to vote, they would have given us candidates'[31]. Not much to add here.

The 2016 list of Republican candidates included the returning favorites Huckabee, Perry and Santorum but they may have become shadows of their former self. Compared to 2012 Rick Santorum caught little media attention and during the debates he never moved out the 'undercard' faction.

He rightfully complained that all the attention went to the 'Trump Show'. Unfortunately, this is what happens when issues, content and focus of news programs are driven by ratings and advertisers.

Then there are the so-called outsiders, meaning candidates who had not held office before like Donald Trump, Ben Carson or Carly Fiorina and some who actually got elected into public office, either in the Senate, like Rubio, Rand or Cruz or even Governors like Christie, Jindal, Kasich or Walker. In total the roster swelled up to 17 candidates by mid of 2015. Let us have a closer look at some of the bunch of contenders.

Bobby Jindal, who never got anywhere in the polls, left the race before anyone had a chance noticing that he was actually running.

---

[31] Quelle: Jim Hightower: If the gods had meant us to vote, they would have given us candidates

Rick Perry was the first one to leave the race, before he even did or said something worth mentioning. It is said he ran out of funds to keep his campaign operating. Maybe he just forgot what he was running for.

John Kasich of Ohio, by far the most moderate and probably most qualified Republican Presidential candidate, clearly brought some much needed common sense to the Republican debates. He was also the one who realized early on that the Presidency would be handed to the Democrats as long as some of his contenders acted like maniacs. After winning his home state of Ohio he may well be one of the candidates heading into a contested convention.

Senator Ted Cruz is one of the guys from the far right corner. When it came to the immigration issue energized by the refugee crisis in Europe and the assaults in Paris he showed his human side. Instead of the 10,000 refugees a year the Obama administration wanted to take up, just a notch short of the daily influx into Germany at that time, or the 65,000 a year Hillary Clinton and Bernie Saunders offered, he also opened his heart and, if elected, also wanted to let refugees enter the United States, as long as they were Christians.

Although he proposed a path into legality for illegal immigrants in the just recent past he now is going with the conservative flow of being strongly against any legal status. He is against same-sex marriage and encourages states to just ignore the ruling of the Supreme Court[32].

He also wants to abolish the IRS. Although he chairs the Subcommittee on Space, Science and Competitiveness, he could not be called a friend of science. He wanted to stop NASA from analyzing climate change and temperatures on earth.

On guns he states that the right to bear arms makes Americans the ´ultimate check against governmental tyranny´. This brings to memory the contrary but sane action by former President George H.W. Bush, who quit the NRA in 1995 after the main voice of gun rights called federal agents ´jack-booted jugs´[33]. Speaking of arms; Ted Cruz wants to carpet bomb Syria, but only hitting the bad guys from IS. Must be some carpet!.

Senator Rand Paul is a self-acclaimed libertarian walking in the shoes of his famed father, who just gave it another try four years earlier. Rand Paul is kind of a bird of paradise among his fellow Republicans and got noticed for his stand on international agreements.

He is known to block double taxation treaties (DTT) moving to the Senate floor thus preventing a vote on such agreements. Some DTT with countries like Luxembourg or Switzerland were pending in limbo for

---

[32] Source: The Economist, November 14, 2015

[33] Source: Newsweek, August 21, 2015

many years just one guy wanted to make a point and some strange rules allowed it.

He also used any political means to stop or, once it passed anyway, to repeal the Foreign Account Tax Compliance Act (FATCA[34]). He is against FATCA because he does not want financial information on foreigners holding accounts in the U.S. sent overseas.

If he would have the same pity for Americans who live overseas and whose financial information banks around the globe have to send to the IRS, directly or indirectly, his stand would be more honorable.

As FATCA now stands, the United States merely delivers some interest and dividend payments, if anything at all, to some selective countries where reciprocal agreements are in place, whereas the ′Rest of the World′ has to deliver the full load of financial information to the U.S. turning ′reciprocal′ into a joke.

The U.S. is also one of the very, very few countries refusing to participate in the automatic exchange of information aka the Common Reporting Standard (CRS) introduced by the OECD. Did we already talk about double standards?

Carly Fiorina turned out to be the only woman on the Republican ticket. Like a few on the roster, she has no political experience at all but

---

[34] Source: Karlheinz Moll: FATCA – Wenn der Fiskus zweimal klingelt, 2014

seems to think a country can be run like a tech company. Someone who set a price of a toner cartridge or sold some printers in another life may also be qualified brokering an atomic deal with Iran or deal with a crisis in the Chinese Seas.

In the second debate she tried to make a point that she would be tough as nails as Commander in Chief. She stated she would take it up with Vladimir Putin by sending 5,000 troops to Germany to be stationed at the border to Poland. At least this is what her advisors must have whispered into her ears and what she so perfectly memorized for her stage time on TV.

What those ghost whisperers did not tell her and what Fiorina may have missed in her time in school that Germany is a sovereign country where you can´t just drop some U.S. troops on the ground.

She may not have been elected so far into office, but then she did not much voting herself either. It came out that she did not vote in state elections for the better of 10 years while living in New Jersey and needed a lot of public convincing to start voting once she moved to California where she did not vote during her first six years there either. Made it even harder considering to vote for her.

Carly Fiorina mentioned the 73,000 pages of the U.S. internal revenue code and her plans to reduce it to 3 simple pages. Most would agree that an overhaul of the tax code is long overdue. Most would probably also agree that it would take a rather long time to make sure that all subsidies, write-offs, tax credits, exchange-in-kinds and many more goodies which are embedded in the internal revenue code could be eliminated on which every American is counting-on one way or the other. Only very few would believe that a reduced tax code could fit on 3 pages even in the best of intentions. Her game was over after New Hampshire.

One of the big names on the ticket turned out to be another one from the Bush dynasty. Jeb Bush, son of former President George H.W., who, in my opinion did a much better job as President as history wants to portray him, and brother of the simple minded George W., who also tried to be a successful, well remembered President. But hey, who´s perfect? At least he tried.

Surprisingly Jeb called it quits after the primary in South Carolina. Like John Kasich he was a rather moderate candidate and also brought experience to the table not to forget the whole Republican network of his father and W. Maybe he was just following the advice of his mother Barbara who said ´We´ve had enough Bushes´.

That reminds me of a story once told by the former German Foreign Minister, Hans-Dietrich Genscher, overhearing a story at the Bush ranch back when George H.W. was Vice President in the Reagan Administration. Reporters asked him about his sons and whether we could imagine anyone of them could ever become President. At this moment Barbara

Bush interfered by saying ´not him´, pointing to George W. Some of us would probably wish she were right[35].

Scott Walker, another Governor, had pretty good cards for a while so it came as a surprise how fast he left the race. Obviously he was burning cash much faster than donors were able to refill his war chest.

The next in line has no political experience either or held any public office. Former surgeon Ben Carson appears like a soft spoken charismatic candidate, not the yelling kind of type. When asked what on earth was driving him when considering running for President with no political experience at all and who never held any office? He claims that God would enable his Presidential run. Obviously that did not happen.

One of his strange conclusions were that the Holocaust would not have turned out so bad for the Jews in the Third Reich if they would just had owned guns and were packing heat. Ben Carson may have a vast network and contact among neuro surgeons but he seems to lack a team of experts and peers in the political field.

This let to statements like during one of the debates in November 2015 when he suggested that China would already be actively involved in the civil war in Syria. It caused the Chinese government as well as American officials to denounce such nonsense.

---

[35] Source: Süddeutsche Zeitung Magazin

And then there is the He-Man on the list of Republican Candidates, Donald – The Donald – Trump. When he entered the race in 2015 many, including me, thought this is just a short stunt to promote his TV show or a new book. He is the only candidate fully financing his campaign on his own. If he really owns that billion he claims to have? Probably only his accountants know.

The core of Trump´s supporters are white, conservative, not overly religious, rather high school than college, looking for better jobs, or any job, and in general people who again want an America like back in the good old days, whenever that was.

On immigration, he limited himself to building a high, ´beautiful´ wall alongside the Mexican border and generally declaring illegal immigrants as criminals and rapists. This may not sit well with the ´Hispanics´ who are a deciding factor in many elections and, if the predictions come true, will surpass the majority of the U.S. population as early as the mid of the 21st century. The Donald also wants to prevent any Muslim from entering the United States. It seems that the inscription on Lady Liberty needs to be expanded. It might then say ´Give me your tired, poor…as long as they are not Muslims´.

On foreign policy, he would just sit down with Vladimir Putin and talk some sense into him or suggested to bomb Syria into kingdom come. The world can be so simple if reality is put to rest. He also dared mentioning that 9/11 happened on George W's watch and that he was responsible for the WMD fiasco in Iraq.

The Donald also has his view on guns. Although he is from New York and his views were way more moderate just a while back. During one of the Republican debates in 2015, just shortly after the Paris attacks when France mourned the victims and started finding out how these people got a hold on guns, Donald Trump said 'if they had guns on the other side...you wouldn't have 130 people plus dead'. He might have been right; the carnage could had been much greater if 130 people plus, with more or less, more likely no experience in firing a gun on moving targets in a fearful situation, would have started firing wildly into the crowd.

Donald Trump beat Marco Rubio in Florida. After March 15, only three contenders were still standing. At Easter the primaries reached a stage where Cruz, Kasich and Trump might straightly heading into a contested convention.

What all these candidates have in common; they are good for some entertainment. In some way it is a modern version of the old Roman 'Panem et Circenses' (Bread and Games) approach were the ordinary people were kept off the streets by luring them to the Coliseum or the Circus Maximus way back in another time.

The Democrats not only offered a very short list of candidates. The roster also did not even get close to the three-ring-circus the Republicans brought to town. Hillary Clinton was considered a candidate a long time before she finally announced to run. There is not much to tell about her what has not already been told hundreds of times before, be it as First Lady, Senator or Secretary of State. The Republicans had a field day with her actions in the Benghazi incident dragging her to numerous congressional hearings.

It would had been interesting to see if the U.S. Congress would have shown the same level of enthusiasm and endurance getting to the bottom of the intelligence that led to the attack, invasion and occupation of Iraq and elected officials ordering to torture anyone at will, even U.S. Citizens, under the flag of patriotism instead of letting those responsible enjoying their retirement in the sun.

Some Republicans may still believe they got another ´scandal´ to pin on her private e-mail account. Some may wonder, why those hundreds of public officials who have probably sent e-mails to her account or responded to her correspondence did not raise concerns or complains about the usage of a private e-mail account while she was in office. Maybe it was not important back then because she did not run for President.

It took her direct opponent Bernie Sanders to put an end to this when he made his point during two Democratic debates that he and the people had enough of talking about her e-mail account. At least the e-mails were no longer an issue during the Democratic primaries. It has to be seen what is going to happen after the conventions when the Democratic and Republican nominees are facing each other.

Bernie Sanders, who calls himself a socialist Democrat appears like a man from another time. Soft spoken like Ben Carson but with experience and what he says and want is well considered and based on facts though not everyone will agree with his plans. But his basic ideas are not far from those of Hillary Clinton, like asking for a share fair from the top 1 percent. It has to be seen how long he will be able to stay in the race.

Movie Recommendations:
- *My fellow Americans starring mit James Garner*

27.   Measles are for everyone

There are diseases which should be extinct in a medically well-organized world. Measles should be one of those diseases gone by now, at least in the western hemisphere. This was true for the United States where 90% of the population was vaccinated against measles until recently.

But these days seem to be over. Some conservative circles use the media which again infects some politicians and in the end symptoms are trickling through to ordinary citizens. It reached a state where an increasing portion of the population seems to believe now that vaccinations would be another attempt by the federal government to take away yet another piece of freedom from the people. The Donald belongs to the fraction heating up the steam.

It seems to be increasingly simple to win over a fraction of the people for almost anything as long as it ends up battling Washington. Obamacare and Obamacore send their humble greetings.

Thanks to this development, the vaccination rates are practically in free fall. The vaccination rate against measles has reached 80%, going south. Outbreaks of measles come naturally now, early 2015 in Disneyland for example. There is no better place to spread decease than an amusement park packed with children. Enjoy the rides!

It is also quite interesting what some of the parents use in front of a camera[36] as arguments not having their kids vaccinated any longer. Expressing individual freedom makes it to the top of the list. When being asked about their opinions, what would happen if their unvaccinated kid would infect others the simple response was that it would be unfortunate but submitting deceases to others is less important than individual freedom. Stay healthy!

Movie Recommendations:
- *Contagion starring Matt Damon*

---

[36] Source: Weltspiegel

28. And then there were Nine

The extreme political polarization that is going on in Washington for so many years has by now crippled the U.S. Congress causing that the population rates the trust in the institution at a historically low level of 10%.

Even routine actions like the annual budget or inevitably increasing the debt limit make it to the voting floor and only get approved after long negotiations and medial showdowns. If it becomes increasingly difficult to reach common ground in Congress on day-to-day decisions it seems to be almost impossible reaching decisions on things that really matter.

So what do some parties do when they can't succeed with their agenda; say repealing Obamacare or putting a stop to Gay Marriage? They are trying anything up their sleeves in Congress, mobilizing easy bending media outlets and creating moral uproar among a concerned and frightened population.

If those initiatives are not successful they start digging in law books and regulations to find anything that could loosely be in violation of the Constitution. After that it directly leads to the Hopeful Nine.

The Nine are the judges elected for life presiding over the Supreme Court. The Supreme Court, even publicly voiced by some of its honorable members, are increasingly being used as some sort of lawmaking institution rather than ensuring that laws enacted are in line with the Constitution and thus far away from what the founding fathers had in mind establishing the highest court in the U.S.

Nonetheless, the Supreme Court has to wade through piles of briefs on issues that should normally be dealt with by the elected officials during those few days they are not campaigning. It so happened with Obamacare and Gay Marriage.

Both issues, a close call as in most cases the highest court has to deal with, will have long lasting effects on the U.S. society, just like other court decisions had in the past. Think of opening the floodgates on gun ownership allowing almost anyone owning assault style guns as if this would have been what the founding fathers intended.

The decisions on socialized health insurance and gay marriage may have some advantages though. For the media and the political class these topics have now lost their appeal and they have to move on to greener pastures. Most Republican Candidates are probably happy about it to got rid of those hot issues although some, Ted Cruz comes to mind, seem to play with the idea moving into another battle, provided they get elected. Even then, trying to change the Constitution is close of being impossible considering the divided Congress. So we can only look forward to the next issues the magnificent nine have to deal with.

With topics like these to deal with, some of the judges might wish the tenure would not be for life.

It will have to be seen how the nominee of President Obama, Merrick Garland, who in the past received praise by many Republicans will play out and how the ultimate successor of the late Antonin Scalia will impact upcoming rulings of the Supreme Court.

Movie and TV Recommendations:
- *Ten little Indians starring Walter Huston*
- *Dress Gray starring Alec Baldwin*

Part IV

Showtime

29. Left, right and in-between

There is barely any subject where the controversies of the United States are more visible at play than on those TV channels that call themselves news media. As in the political arena, these news stations can be clearly separated by political affiliation mirroring the division of the population, even though the stations would probably not admit it.

It all started in 1987 when the news media could change its rules. From now on news outlets were no longer required to provide neutral news coverage. It opened Pandora´s box to polarized news media allowing some of them offering one-sided information, mangled truths and flat-out lies. In every corner of the political spectrum there is a news program catering to its flock 24/7 leaving little room for balanced opinions and common sense.

It is said that the truth is the first victim in any war. Although the United States are in no official state of war with any country, besides the on-going military adventures in Afghanistan, Iraq or Syria, truth was recused to a supporting role long ago on selective TV news outlets and in the parallel universe of talk radio. The result is a type of mass psychology

Gustave Le Bon[37] has so perfectly studied, explored and published at the end of the 19th century.

In such media universes there is no place for any shades of grey but just plain black and white. Statements made by those who yell the loudest and whose opinions are the most outrageous have taken the place of investigative journalism, well founded news analysis and, in the originally intended sense, neutral and balance reporting on global, national and local level provided by a once proud and devoted news business. But no more!

TV Recommendations:
- *Newsroom starring Jeff Daniels*

---

[37] Source: Gustave Le Bon: Psychology of the Masses

30.   This is CNN

This is CNN! The news station best advertised by the deep, well sounded voice of James Earl Jones. CNN is the mother of all news channels. It was the first famed national and international news station with nothing on air than news only interrupted by the inevitable commercial breaks every few minutes.

Remember the Iraq war? I am not referring to the attack and invasion started by George Junior in 2003 but the U.S. led international coalition built by his father George H.W. Bush, his Secretary of State James Baker and the well-coordinated military response against the invasion of Kuwait by the then Iraqi leader Saddam Hussein.

Those who were old enough to watch the news back then saw daily reports of almost identical pictures which looked straight out of a video game. Although we could barely see anything besides the green and white flashes of missiles and gunfire shot in the dark of the night it felt like being very close to the action in the desert war somewhere between Iraq and Kuwait.

I remember watching the news in the morning every day back then before heading to work, so my only memories of that episode are the live reports from nightly activities. The news material, regardless on which channel it was broadcasted, was provided almost exclusively by CNN.

It where people like Peter Arnett from CNN, who continuously reported from the hot spots in Iraq, long before reporters were reduced to ´embedded journalists´. The coverage of this war maybe was the first big hour of CNN. At least anyone around the globe knew what CNN was.

Then came September 11, 2011, or simply 9/11 and the horror of that day was covered by CNN 24/7. I was in Centralia, south of Olympia in the state of Washington and spent most of the morning hours glued to the TV watching the same pictures of the two planes hitting the towers and the smoke and the rubble over and over. CNN probably reached its highest level of popularity and ratings on 9/11 and in the aftermath.

Bernard Shaw once said something in the sense of ´you can reach the top, but you can´t remain there´ which also became true for CNN. The downturn began with the rise of competing news outlets like Fox News and MSNBC, to just name the most prominent examples, and with it came the polarized news, we had to get used to today.

The rather centered type of reporting could not keep up with the new kids on the block who focused more on opinion and entertainment with little appetite for fact checking and detailed analysis.

To regain lost ground CNN started copying the news style of Fox News while trying to stay in the middle of the public opinion. Something like that would still work out to be a success model in Europe even today, but in the United Sates CNN lost more and more of its appeal.

If you are in Europe and watch CNN on British television with some of their leading voices, notably Richard Quest, you can barely believe that the channels bare the same name. In the UK, like BBC and others, news channels have a different standing and do not have to compete with tabloids making it much more watchable than in the U.S.

If it were not for natural disasters, occasional military campaigns or the mass shooting of the day, topics that CNN knows how to cover, ratings of CNN would be in a dismal state.

CNN adopted the bad habit from other stations picking the topic of the day and milking the subject the whole day in every program and any discussion. So you can switch to CNN any time during the day and still be sure to catch the 'breaking news' of the day until it hits day break where the next subject is already in the waiting. It does not really matter what the issue is. Almost anything can make it to the 'Situation Room' be it a shooting, a legal battle, a political rant or just a dog on the run.

Some of the most prominent faces of CNN in the U.S. are people like Anderson Cooper and Wolf Blitzer and it sometimes feels as those two would be on air all day. Wolf Blitzer heads the so-called 'Situation

Room´, not at all to be mixed up with the real thing in the White House, where real important situations are being covered.

Wolf Blitzer got some unexpected fame on Fox where a character just like him appeared on the TV show ´24´ and where Jack Bauer saved the day once again. In one episode it showed a guy looking much like the original and introduced the news person as ´Wolfgang Blitzkrieg´.

If CNN really has a chance to survive in the middle of the equation and with all the news available on the internet and mobile devices will have to be seen. The chances are rather dim.

Movie and TV Recommendations:
- *Network mit William Holden*
- *24 mit Kiefer Sutherland*

31.   Who let the fox out?

O n the right wing of the equation the entertainment factor has long become the starring actor whereas real news are playing not much more than a small supporting role, provided that you consider the stuff these news channels put on the air entertaining.

At least you do not have to take it seriously what the protagonists, moderators and anchors are serving you each day although the devoted viewers may see that differently. The main news channel on the far right is Fox News, maybe the only TV station which manages to successfully survive in a parallel media universe catering to an audience that is mainly male and white. Exceptions are merely a confirmation to the rule.

According to the Pew Institute Fox News is the prime, and often only, source of news of the population voting Republican. A voluntary media brainwashing whose effects would probably be even more devastating if this modern type of right propaganda camouflaged as journalism would not be interrupted by commercials every few minutes. What might be more numbing? Who could tell?

Dick Cheney, you know the guy who kept beating the drums to the American people, and probably to himself, that Iraq stockpiled weapons of mass destruction and that it was somehow involved in the tragic events and horrors of 9/11. Manipulated information and facts so perfectly orchestrated that some of his dearest followers seem to believe that nonsense up to this very day. Whether that is true for Dick Cheney too has not been reported yet.

Well, this Dick Cheney, while still in office, is said to have insisted that whenever he entered a hotel room, Fox News would had to be switched on TV, nothing else. Whether that is true too or not…who cares?

Most programs and shows on Fox News are following a similar pattern, particularly those shown in the afternoon and the early evening hour, a system that found many copy cats like the aforementioned CNN. The ingredients include a moderator, mostly a white male, who guides through the issue with lots of guests, all of them self-proclaimed experts on the subject of the day, of course.

Those invited typically provide their insights which only marginally differ from the opinion of the moderator, particularly when the likes of Sean Hannity or Bill O´Reilly, more on him later on, are on air, which is basically daily. Any dissent is either cut-off or considered sleeping with the enemy.

Those who would be interested in lively discussions with a broad set of opinions would be wildly disappointed. But no problem there; the majority of the fans of Fox news only want to get a confirmation of what they already believe.

Later in the day on Fox News, when you might think it cannot get much worse, Bill O´Reilly and his daily horror picture show starts.

On first look, the O´Reilly Factor with all its spinning in the zone looks like a normal news program. He sits in a nice studio held in conservative blue, lots of screens and a moderator impersonating as a classic anchor of journalism in the tradition of Dan Rather. But it has nothing to do with news. It is a show at best, like the good old nightly news in Eastern Germany in the 1980s or what you can expect from public news programs in Russia or Poland today. The only difference is that in Russia or Poland it is the government telling the news stations what to broadcast compared to advertisers in America.

His show is watched primarily by white, conservative, Republican voting men. It offers a dim picture of the country worn down by Democrats, liberals and all those millions of Americans not tuning in. In that dark world he considers himself the white knight on an equally white horse holding up the torch of mankind. Watching Bill you can´t help but getting the notion that the country would be at the brink of losing out against a Democratic elite who wants to spread socialism in the United States like Obamacare. He seems to be on a televised mission against anything linked to the federal government and that he will not rest until all the evil in America is put to eternal rest. We sincerely hope he won´t be on air that long.

Where he is big on complaining he comes up mostly empty handed offering solutions or alternatives. This type of show for a very selective clientele has nothing to do with serious journalism but offers perfect entertainment to those who, after a hard day's work, only want to sit back, relax and listen to opinions in sync with their own fenced-in set of mind.

To run a show like this, Bill O´Reilly would not have had to study journalism, reading on mass psychology in the tradition of Gustave Le Bon[38] would had been enough. Important issues and topics which would inform and educate the people are not his thing. He neither wants to bore nor overwhelm his viewers with neutral reports and balanced discussions.

He also helps the audience to easily digest complex global issues like war, hunger, diseases or international finances with simple worlds and suggesting that all troubles of the world could be solved with even simpler but usually drastic solutions, all offered within the hour. Of course he does not need to worry about ever being challenged on anything he said, as he never had or will have to walk the big talk and what he says will be forgotten the next day anyway.

Whenever in the U.S., I cannot help it but to watch his show at least for a few minutes always hoping it got any better or he has already been put off the air. But so far these hopes were not fruitful. I remember a particular episode in 2015 that so perfectly explains the O´Reilly factor. It was

---

[38] Source: Gustave Le Bon: Psychology of the Masses, 1895

about the legal treatment of sexual offenders. Sex and crime is still a steady guarantee of high ratings, even in a news show. In this show he claimed that judges were too soft on sex offenders and needed to be taught a lesson of harsh sentencing. For this discussion we invited some district attorneys to help him explaining the legal proceedings in court.

Bill O'Reilly was not very happy with the way sexual offenders were sentenced. He demanded that all sexual offenders be locked-up for life without parole. What about the type of offense, the circumstances of the crime as well as the motive, history or the psychologic state of mind of the delinquents? Never mind. He asked the two district attorneys what punishment they would consider suitable. They could not help but offering the truth, meaning that the sentence would vary depending on the case and that therapy also would need to be considered.

That, particular the mentioning of therapies, got Bill almost enraged and it was obvious that he was not at least satisfied with these assessments. He waved aside their comments and moved to the next commercial break. I am not sure whether all he does and says is just a role and he is playing the part like a good actor who has to play a bad character although he is a nice guy as soon as the curtain comes down and the light goes out. That he at least must have a different, more centered and likable personality becomes obvious through the numerous history books he co-authored, like 'Killing Patton' or 'Killing Lincoln'.

In his book about `Legends and Lies: The Real West´ he mixed up a few facts though. He told the story of John Henry ´Doc´ Holliday telling Ike Clanton on the night before the gun fight at the OK Corral on October 26, 1881 that he had killed his father his son. But truth has it that Newman H. Clanton was killed on August 13, 1881 during a fight with Mexican troops[39].

There are also quite talented news people at Fox News. Megyn Kelly or Bret Baier are good examples for that. Bret Baier did a great job during the televised debates and town halls, even those with Democrats Hillary Clinton and Bernie Sanders. Megyn Kelly is the new superstar of Fox News and much better looking than Bill O´Reilly. She may be as much as conservative as the rest of the bunch but Megyn Kelly brings certain qualities to the screen. She listens and does not interrupt, regardless of what is being said and whether she agrees with it.

Megyn got to national fame in the 2012 election night when Fox News proclaimed President Obama winner and re-elected while her guest Karl Rove went bananas as he did not want to accept the results while many votes were not counted. Megyn tried to calm him down by convincing him ´He won, Karl, he won´.

She got international attention and recognition through the Republican debates, like the first one on August 6, 2015 moderated by Fox News.

---

[39] Source: B.S. at the OK Corral by Casey Tefertiller published in True West

During the debate and in her program afterwards she obviously asked questions that hit Donald Trump right on his nerves and he really got enraged. What he insinuated would ruin the good nature of this book, so I won't repeat it here. His comments were so far out of line that one of his campaign managers promptly resigned.

Outside the debate circuit Megyn, like Old Bill, runs her own daily show. I noticed that she follows the same patterns, meaning she is covering more or less the same topics her colleagues before and after her slot have on their agenda. Her ratings beat Bill's by length now. At least a refreshing face compared to the dinosaur Bill O'Reilly and we all know what happened to the dinosaurs.

Of course she has her weak moments too. One was in December 2013 when she suggested Santa and Jesus were white skinned fellows. Stephen Colbert commented on that in the sense of 'Megyn likes to put the things into black and white...mostly white'[40]. Later on she watered down her own assessment by stating that their skin color is still unclear. There is hope out there for Fox News.

---

[40] Source: The Huffington Post, 13.12.2013, accessed on August 10, 2015

32. A turn to the Left

Nature has it that once the pendulum swings too far in one direction, the counter swing is not far off. This rule applies to the news media too. As a direct response to Fox News, MSNBC was established to cover the left side of the equation. They actually use the same patterns and cover the same topics as Fox News just the light is coming from a different direction.

What makes this chapter so short is the importance of this left wing news channel. The ratings of MSNBC are no match compared to those of Fox News. One reason behind that is that viewers of MSNBC also switch on to other news providers like CNN.

What can be said though is that MSNBC at least tries not to be overly biased and definitely does a better job researching their material and trying to limit inaccuracies and misinformation.

The moderators are typically well prepared and it is good to watch that most of them are considered moderates allowing other opinions too and the discussions seem to have more depth. Of course that is only a personal observation.

One of the most prominent pendants to the likes of Bill O'Reilly or Megyn Kelly on MSNBC is Rachel Maddow, the star of her daily news show.

She is very intelligent and sharp as a whip. Sometimes though I am amazed how many times she can squeeze the word Republicans into any of her sentences. In the end it is possible to stay tuned a bit longer but switching channels is also inevitable after a while.

To really find unbiased news and political talk on TV without people yelling at each other or simple delivering one-liner, you only have a few choices left. You may want to switch to PBS or even tune into some international channels like BBC.

Movie Recommendations:
-   *The Untouchables starring Robert Redford*

33. Ball Games

For starters, I am not a fan of any ball games, be it Soccer, Football, Baseball or anything else. That is the reason why I don´t even try to argue about it. But there is one story which occurred during the soccer world games 2014 in Rio de Janeiro that is too good not to be covered in this chapter about news.

In America, the way ball sport events like Football and Baseball games are watched and consumed is quite different to Europe where soccer is the prime ball game. Sitting in an American ball park illustrates those differences perfectly and explains in part why it is so difficult for soccer to leave a strong footprint in American sports.

Americans visiting a ball game quite obviously consider it a socializing event where watching the game is only part of the gathering. Equally important seem to be eating, lots of it, and drinking, mainly beer and soft drinks by the gallon.

There is no fear missing any of the action while reloading the food trays and soft drink buckets as the games are constantly interrupted by commercial breaks, entertainment or cheerleaders. I once read that the actual time the players in a 3-hour Superbowl spectacle are really ´in action´ are 25 minutes or less.

In Europe, a 90 minute soccer game is only interrupted once for a 15 minute break. During the game almost no one leaves their seats as an important action can happen any time.

The 2014 soccer world games in Rio had the highest U.S. viewership of a soccer game on TV, even higher than when America hosted the games. There are several reasons for this popularity; immigrants from Middle and South America are probably the most important ones.

So much about some of the differences between the two sports, which Ann Coulter used as a basis for an outrage against soccer. For those who don´t know her or have never heard of her, Ann Coulter is an ultra-conservative columnist and book author with thrilling titles like ´If the Democrats had any brains, they would be Republicans´. Like Bill O´Reilly, it is not entirely clear why she is playing the fiddle for the extreme right.

The game between Portugal and the United States was watched by a whopping 18 million Americans. It may be whopping for a soccer game, but just the normal viewership of a NFL game on any given Sunday. But the media were full of enthusiasm about the increased popularity of soccer games.

Anyway, Ann Coulter used this game to start a mission against soccer in general and fans of the game in particular. She referenced the 18 million viewer of the game against Portugal to the 111 million watching the

Super Bowl. It still beats me what she wanted to achieve with that fact? Is she concerned that soccer becomes increasingly popular and could surpass football? Even if that would be the case in a few decades, does it matter? Probably not!

She went on saying that the era of Ted Kennedy would be to blame for the increased interest in soccer because he was one of the initiators of an immigration reform in 1965 allowing more people coming into the country.

In other words, would America had let less foreigners immigrate to the Unites States since then, there would be less soccer fans today. Now we are getting closer.

Intended or coincidentally she is firing up the fear from other, foreign people with different values and believes who watch un-American sports. She should not be scared; soccer is just a game.

Later on she said that soccer would be a women's sport. She should have said, soccer is also a women's sport, especially in the U.S. The women soccer team won the third consecutive world games in July 2015.

She also compared the players by saying that the beefed-up football players who at best leave the field heavily bruised on a stretcher whereas soccer players are just running around and in the end it may end in an even game. In her small world, there must always be a winner.

Her rants were so outrageous that even some moderators on Fox News were puzzled what seems to be driving her. Maybe we are better off not knowing.

From the beginning of the 2016 Presidential election circus, Ann Coulter supported Donald Trump. After the Paris attacks she claimed that the deadly incident ´just got Donald Trump elected President´. Later on she proclaimed that God had sent Donald Trump to save America from destruction.

This caused even the most conservative news talkers to raise their voice. Steve Deace, another ultra-conservative talk-radio host, who wants to save America from all evils, three hours a day at a time, strongly disagreed with her because he does not consider Donald an authentic candidate.

Movie Recommendations:
- *Field of Dreams starring Kevin Costner*
- *Leatherheads starring mit George Clooney*
- *Major League starring Tom Berenger*

34. Celluloid Dreams

I f there is one cultural product which is inevitably linked to the United States it is Hollywood and its Movie and TV industry. Many tried to copy it but even today no country comes even close to the movie and television production industry of Hollywood.

Film cameras and film material were barely invented when the first movie productions were launched. These are the 1890s we are talking about. While the Wild West was riding into the sundown, the East already started filming the legend.

In the years when Butch Cassidy and the Sundance Kid of the ´Wild Bunch´ were still robbing banks and trains, the film company of Thomas Edison already produced the first short movies like ´Sioux Ghost Dance´ or the 30 second blockbuster ´Buffalo Bill – The noted proprietor of the wild west´ shot 1894 starring William Frederic Cody alias Buffalo Bill and his Wild West Circus.

Buffalo Bill on the other hand was working for the U.S. Cavalry fighting Indians in the years following the battle at the Little Big Horn just 20 years earlier.

The seamless, sometimes overlapping times between the remainders of the western frontier and the modern times help to explain the glorification of historic people.

Famous people from the old west like Wyatt Earp, Frank James or Emmett Dalton, whose members of the Dalton gang were shot during a bank robbery in Coffeyville 1892, survived the wild times and lived far into the 20th century.

They basically were the makers of their own legend. The glory stories they told news reporters and book authors helped building the legends of these historic figures making it difficult to know what truly happened and what was exaggerated or simply made up. Unfortunately the stories on Wyatt Earp, who worked and liaised with cowboy stars from the silent era like Tom Mix, had its breakthrough in movies after the famed lawman passed away.

Movie Recommendations:
- *Butch Cassidy and Sundance Kid starring Robert Redford*
- *Butch and Sundance – The early years starring Tom Berenger*
- *Buffalo Bill starring Joel McCrea*

35. The Roaring Twenties

I n the blossoming years of the talking pictures at the end of the 1920s, Hollywood productions were completely uncontrolled and uncensored. The movie makers had full creative freedom and the moviegoers got what they wanted.

There were no boundaries what could be put on celluloid at least until 1934. The talking pictures made between 1929 and 1933 are called pre-code thus the years before a codex defined what is morally accepted to show on a movie screen.

When the movies learned to talk, Hollywood put their top stars of the time in gangster roles and dramas that often provided examples where being or becoming a criminal was a career option or being morally corrupted would be an acceptable way to fame and success.

At that time movie stars were role models for many, just the way some are today. Adding to it the fact that movies were the prime media source back then and it was not uncommon watching multiple movies on any given weekend.

Leading ladies of the time like Norma Shearer, Mae West or Barbara Stanwyck played shady characters and femme fatales. Men like Joel

McCrea, Clark Gable or Warren William portrayed gangsters or corrupt personalities.

The big gangster movie stars of the time like James Cagney or Edward G. Robinson played successful career mobsters in the years of the Great Depression.

Then there were the comedies, where some actors played so relaxed and coy that viewers could get the impression, they had a stiff drink too many or smoked some weed before stepping in front of the camera. Some of these early screwball comedies with William Powell, Cary Grant or Jean Arthur were immensely popular.

Not to forget nudity or clad clothing on screen. Make no mistake; there was not much nudity at all, particularly not to the extent what we are used to today. A famous example is the swimming scene with Tarzan and Jane in the second Tarzan movie starring Johnny Weissmuller which caught the attention of the moral apostils.

It were those type of movies which led to a self-imposed codex by the movie industry, the so-called Production Code, sometimes mixed-up with the earlier Hays Code on which the Production Code was based. Under the code, leading actors continued playing gangsters or femme fatales but the scrips had no more happy-ends for them.

Gangsters had to die in the end or end up in prison. Bedrooms got a moral makeover with separated beds and long nightgowns. It took another 30 years to bring back some of that cinematographic liberty.

Movie Recommendations:
- *Baby Face starring Barbara Stanwyck*
- *The Thin Man starring William Powell*
- *The Public Enemy starring James Cagney*
- *Tarzan and his mate starring Johnny Weissmueller*

36.   Depression, War and Baby Boomers

I n the depression years of the 1930s and during the World War II years cinemas were a place for escapism. At least once a week Americans wanted to distance from the economic misery and, after Pearl Harbor, the war. Particularly, it were the Screwball comedies that boomed during those years and many movies of that time became classics which have not lost its appeal today.

Then there were western, produced on a budget but fast paced and action packed which were part of the weekly line-up of a Saturday matinee and plenty of war movies loaded with propaganda providing moral support for the fight against Germany and Japan.

After the war movie screens became more colorful with the breakthrough of Technicolor and, with the introduction the Cinemascope, broader. Even black and white movies were still doing well, especially the so-called 'film noir'. The period produced some of the best movies of all time and helped carrying a positive image of the United States around the globe that lasted for many years.

Television became a mass media in the 1950s and was soon competing with movie theaters. After the late 1940s and early 1950s, the program was mainly made of game shows, news programs, western movies with singing cowboys for kids and some crime shows. During the second half of the 1950s adult TV shows became increasingly popular.

The 1950s also brought a magazine for all those hungry for investigative journalism and high class interviews only briefly interrupted by some nude pictures. A Norma Jean Baker came to first fame as a Playboy centerfold before becoming a movie star under her new name Marilyn Monroe.

Movie Recommendations:
- *Too many Husbands starring Fred MacMurray*
- *The Philadelphia Story starring Cary Grant*
- *The more the merrier starring Jean Arthur*
- *To Catch a Thief starring Cary Grant*
- *Brining up Baby starring Cary Grant*

37. James Bond and Mini Skirts

Television surpassed movie theaters as the main source of entertainment in the course of the 1960s. People stayed home more often to enjoy the ever expanding program offering of the main networks.

The budgets of the TV shows increased constantly and the networks started showing made-for-TV movies in direct competition to the cinema. Some of these series enjoyed equal popularity around the globe. The family oriented western series `Bonanza` hit the top spot of the Nielsen ratings for many years in the U.S. as it did in many other countries.

The movie industry reacted to the competition by changing the pace and content of the movies. Crime movies were enriched with lots of action and nudity, western movies became more violent and drama covered darker and controversial issues of the time that were still too hot for TV.

Hollywood was also influenced by Europe, where European co-productions were produced in large quantities. Many of those movies, mostly B-movies compared to U.S. standards, made it to America, like the Karl May adaptations, historic adventure films or the hundreds of so-called Spaghetti western, which were mostly co-productions of many European countries and primarily filmed in Spain.

. The lead was typically played by an American B-movie actor like Lex Barker, Guy Madison, Rory Calhoun or Rod Cameron or an actor previously on the Hollywood A-list but whose peak times had past, like Stewart Granger.

The increasing success of the James Bond franchise even triggered a flood of U.S. spy and secret agent movies, many of them parodies of James Bond movies, like the Derek Flint or Matt Helm films.

Long before outsourcing of labor intensive processes became popular, U.S. movie producers started shooting pictures in Europe. American westerns were increasingly shot in Spain, where European crews shooting Spaghetti westerns could be hired on a budget. Asia, particularly the Philippines, also became a popular location for war and jungle adventures.

The production costs were much lower than in the United States and the favorable exchange rate against foreign currencies made foreign productions a lucrative investment.

Take the example of ´The Treasure of the Silver Lake´ (Der Schatz im Silbersee), a German A-movie, co-produced with other European countries and shot in the mountainous region of Croatia starring the former Tarzan actor Lex Barker.

This European western, the most expensive German movie that time, cost USD 1 million, less than what most American B-movies of that time cost. Compare that to the adaption of Cleopatra starring Elisabeth Taylor which cost a whopping USD 44 million.

Movie and TV Recommendations:
- *Our Man Flint starring James Coburn*
- *The Wrecking Crew starring Dean Martin*
- *Treasure of the Silver Lake starring Lex Barker*
- *Bonanza starring Michael Landon*
- *For a few Dollars more starring Clint Eastwood*

38.   No clothing – No pathos

The early 1970s brought further changes to the movie industry. The civil unrest of the 1960s, the so-called sexual revolution and the long and devastating Vietnam War had a lasting effect on Hollywood.

The sexual freedom, temporally overcoming the notorious American prudency for a few years, caused that nudity on a movie screen became as natural as, well, nudity is. Even A-stars of the era like Jane Fonda, Angie Dickinson or Faye Dunaway had not issue taking their clothes off in front of a movie camera.

The good guys in action movies and western became disillusioned and violent, sometimes barely separable from the bad guys, maybe a direct response to the state of mind of the society.

The Vietnam War with thousands of American GI carried home in body bags, all captured and showed on TV, left scars on the people following the events in the news. Like so often, the hundred thousands of victims on the other side and a country contaminated by Agent Orange was barely worth a footnote, which was also true for the My Lai massacre which caused little uproar and produced practically no learning curve as the horror and cruelty of Abu Ghraib, Guantanamo or the Rendition program proved just 30 years later.

The population back then was politically more interested, active and involved than today. Investigative journalism had its brightest hours. TV news focused on informing people rather than entertaining and the movies of the time were also often influenced by the political developments, reaching its peak with the Watergate affair.

The coverage of the Vietnam War carried the carnage and insanity of the bloodshed almost uncensored into the homes in American. The pictures of body bags brought home from the war zone helped strengthen the anti-war movement. In stark contrast to today, almost every family was somehow affected by the war, had to mourn losses or at least knew others who did.

The relentless coverage of the war and the presidential campaign even toppled President Richard Nixon. There is no much talk about Watergate today, with the exception that the word ′gate′ is commonly attached to many ′affairs′, trying to turning issues of any size and importance into a similar state affair as Watergate.

So we are regularly entertained with new ′gates′, like Irangate (Iran-Contra-Affair – at least as big as Watergate but times had already changed and the issue just faded into history), Monicagate (The Monica Lewinsky Affair – Nothing spectacular on this side of the ocean but enough for

America to almost impeach a President), Troopergate (Even Sarah Palin was honored with her own Alaska affair) or Emailgate (Hilary Clinton using a private E-Mail account/server through which probably thousands of people sent E-Mails without complaining, before she was running for President).

The movie theaters responded in various ways to the diminishing audience and the strong competition from television. In the early 1970s cinema owners split their formerly large theaters into ever smaller cubicles. This explains why many movies of that time were no longer produced in Cinemascope format 2.25:1 but in formats better fitting the small screens like 1.85:1 or 1.67:1.

The 1970s also brought back family oriented TV formats, itself a clear sign that the people needed some escape from the dim reality of war and corruption. Crime shows started to focus more on the lead characters away from gory details of the crime. In general, police work on TV became more colorful, like the clothing of that time.

Satire and crude humor also had its share as the recent DVD release of the ´Dean Martin Celebrity Roast´ shows, which ran from the early seventies into the eighties. Dean Martin hosted an irregular humorous show to honor the ´Man/ Woman of the Day´.

The shows were well scripted and all of the presenters delivered a monologue ´roasting´ the Star as well as the fellow presenters. To describe the humor as crude would mean downplaying what really happened. Political correctness was not invented yet, so the audience, most episodes were taped in Las Vegas, were laughing out loud on religious, racial or political comments which are banned from free TV today. Even Bill Maher sounds like a chorus boy compared to what the likes of Dean Martin, Milton Berle or Don Rickles rattled out, very often reading from cue cards.

Dean Martin even made jokes about the cue cards, if he could not clearly read it.

Movie and TV Recommendations:
- *Big Bad Mama starring Angie Dickinson*
- *Dirty Harry starring Clint Eastwood*
- *Klute starring Jane Fonda*
- *Network starring William Holden*
- *Dean Martin Celebrity Roast starring Dean Martin*

39. Throne Games and Supermen

T he 21st Century brought another revolution to the film and television world. Digital effects and animation have changed movie productions as well as creative writers did for TV series. Add another couple hundred million production costs, the only hurdle for a movie or a TV show to take is the verdict of the paying audience.

Blockbuster movies ensured the survival of the big production companies in the first 15 years of the new century. A perfect example for that are the superhero movies based on DC and Marvel comic book characters. Where is was difficult in the 1970s and 1980s to let superheroes like Batman or Superman do all those things on screen and to let the action scenes appear as realistic as they do in the comic books, modern technology and digital inventions made that all possible.

The TV series made an ever bigger hump. The expansion of pay TV, the sale of DVD and Blue Ray and the constantly increasing downloads and streaming offerings helped producing high quality and very expensive TV series appealing to a global audience.

Regardless what genre, the scripts are often complex, interesting and entertaining and are played out by gifted actors. Of course all the money in the world can't buy success. In average 85% or all TV series that are being produced don´t see the end of the first season. But this seems to be the secret of the success of all good products; it requires a lot of failure to end up with high quality productions. You probably can imagine how many million Dollars are flooded down the drain while trying to produce a successful show.

As there can´t just be high priced, first rated productions to fill the hundreds of TV stations with 24 hours of programming all and every day, an almost unlimited quantity of cheaply produced ´scripted reality´ shows spread out like a contagious disease around the globe.

Whether it be pawn shop operators, producers of whistles for the duck hunt, some frustrated housewives or men and women that, although be accompanied by the whole production crew, are running naked and afraid through unknown wilderness, they want to make the viewers believe that what they are being shown has anything to do with reality. The shows move from one triviality to another with stories the world does not need but the low budgets, mostly cheaply paid ´actors´ and the high revenues from commercials make those productions a million dollar business.

The advantage of such shows is that they don´t require any intellectual pre-requisites. As it seems, scripted reality shows are watched by all fractions of the population, offering another layer of escapism after a hard day´s work.

For whom should we have more pity? The people who have to produce this televised garbage or those watching it. Even though America only knows winners, maybe there is none to this contest.

If you look at movie posters or watch a movie trailer these days, I am not sure whether you check the ratings. I am not referring to the capital letters like R or PG-13 but the texts underneath. The people writing those short texts need to be very creative and inventive alike. Maybe you have noted such quotations like 'language', which obviously is not referring to a foreign language, or 'a scene of sensuality', which might be anything from a stolen kiss in the dark to experimenting with the full fifty shades of grey and 'drug use', which today probably includes smoking a cigarette.

While the movie business reaches new heights, the good old Playboy got rid of the centerfolds, picturing Pamela Anderson once more, so men won't get interrupted anymore while soaking-in artsy articles and interviews.

Movie and TV Recommendations:
- *Batman Begins starring Christian Bale*
- *Game of Thrones starring Sean Bean*
- *Iron Man starring Robert Downey Jr.*
- *Boston Legal starring William Shatner*

Part V

Law and Order

40.   In the Name of Justice

Do you like American movies and series, where the police work or legal proceedings are the focus of the action? Do you know Law & Order or Boston Legal? Such shows leave the impression of a highly developed police, judicial and legal system, where justice always prevails, one way or the other. But movies and TV shows are not always mirroring the reality. Following real legal cases in American media, particularly capital cases, it sometimes appears as if they were a competition where a winner is to be chosen rather than exposing the truth or achieving justice. It surely, or at least thankfully, is not that extreme all the time.

But it seems to happen that a career driven district attorney only presents evidence in court speaking against the defendant while keeping relieving evidence covered-up. If such a smart professional opposes an inexperienced defense lawyer the fate of the defendant might fade away. The established democratic processes is meant to balance overstretched holes in the legal system. At least that is what we are being told, while reality often tells different stories and delivers plenty of reasons to better not getting in conflict with the law. This includes foreigners while visiting the United States. This also goes even if you like to wear overalls and you consider orange being the new black.

Let us start with some splitting hair. Recently the FBI has published a large scale internal review of the reliability of hair samples[41][42]. The FBI found out that matched hair samples used in criminal cases were often unreliable or even faulty. Of the 268 legal cases reviewed, where faulty forensic hair samples played a crucial role, 95% were to the advantage of the state attorneys, led to wrong conclusions and, in extreme cases, caused a sentencing of an innocent defendant.

It is even more disturbing that in 32 of those cases faulty hair samples caused the defendants being sentenced to death. Some of them spent years, in some cases decades, in prison before their innocence were proven. In 14 of those cases even that came too late as they were already executed or died behind bars. Not all such cases are being fully analyzed yet and there is hope that a hair sample was not the only evidence being used in a case and that there were other things proving guilt or innocence of a defendant. But there is hope for the future, that modern DNA technique will someday soon replace the antiquated way of matching hair samples under a microscope, which could then become the only deciding evidence in a capital case.

---

[41] Source: National Association of Criminal Defense Lawyers and the Innocence Project

[42] Source: Washington Post: FBI admits flaws in hair analysis over decades, accessed on April 21, 2015

41. We got him

What we human beings see and perceive is sometimes deceiving, particularly in extreme situations, where we are scared or where our adrenaline level is high up in motion. This is also true, even in everyday, normal moments, where we are occupied with ourselves and our surroundings, out of which we are suddenly pulled out because we are witnessing an accident or, more disturbingly, a crime like a robbery, a fight, a shooting or an assault.

Eye witnesses are often a crucial element in solving a crime and can be the deciding factor in the sentencing of a defendant. Someone witnessing a crime should therefore be pretty confident bevor identifying a person. That is where it is getting complicated.

We humans are easily deceivable and our memory sometimes plays tricks on us, particularly about details of what other people did while a crime was happening. An uncertain recollection of events can lead to a wrong sentencing, which may cost a defendant his freedom or, if it happens in the U.S., even his life.

How good are our observation skills? There is plenty of research out there. All of them came to the same conclusion. Only in rare cases were the statements of eyewitness a reliable and accurate source of information.

During an experiment in 1974, a TV program was shown to a selected crowd: The viewers could watch a staged robbery on a street. In a clip that lasted about 13 seconds, the presumed robber could be clearly seen. After that, six persons were presented to the audience in a row and the viewers were asked to identify the robber. The psychology professor Robert Buckhout summarized the result by saying ´2,000 witnesses can be wrong´. Only 14% of the witnesses got it right! A result that is not easy to swallow, particularly if it would had been a real case.

It can only be guessed how many people are sitting behind bars, or died behind the same, due to wrong or insufficient evidence. Of course there is no reason to suspect massive malpractice in court. The American justice system should be considered too stable for that. However, every single case, where wrong evidence let to a conviction, is one too many.

In an internal review in the state of Pennsylvania it was revealed that 11 people were released from prison during the last 10 years because their innocence could be proven through DNA tests[43]. Those 11 people spent a total of 139 years behind bars. In the majority of cases, wrong identification by eye witnesses were the prime cause of final sentencing.

But change is on the rise. In line-ups, it is increasingly common that all the candidates lined up are looking at least similar to the description of the witness, making a simple identification more difficult and it requires more

---

[43] Source: The Innocence Project: White Paper no Conviction Integrity Proposals on Pennsylvania

concentration and confidence from the witness. In addition, instead of lining up five or six people in a row, the candidates appear ´on stage´ one by one, relieving the tension from the witnesses having to ´pick´ one.

Further on, the police is requested to no longer give ´tips´ that the line-up includes a suspect, making the witness believe that the suspect is already more or less charged and the identification would be a mere formality and letting the identification process appear less serious. Witnesses need to be made aware that their role is not to identify suspects but to point out the person they watched committing a crime, as long as that person is among the line-up.

Movie Recommendations:
- *Trial starring Glenn Ford*
- *Twelve Angry Men starring Henry Fonda*
- *The Runaway Jury starring John Cusack*
- *The big shot starring Humphrey Bogart*

42. Horse-trading behind bars

Tv shows and movies have made us all familiar with a part of the American justice system that includes 'negotiations' outside the courtroom. At the end of such 'trading activities' a defendant confesses to some or all of the charges against him, regardless whether he really committed any crime, with the goal of receiving a lower sentencing and preventing the case from going to court. These proceedings are called 'plea bargains'. Let us take an example to illustrate this strange kind of bazar trading.

Imagine a person, with or without previous record, walks into a gas station, threatens the clerk behind the counter, steals food and cleans out the register on the way out. When the police arrives they not only find a robbed but also a dead cashier. The next day, the robber is captured because a witness saw him entering and leaving the gas station and he is charged with robbery and murder.

Let us assume further that no murder weapon was found neither in the gas station nor in the possession of the person charged and that there was no physical evidence linking the robber firmly with the murder except that he was at the scene of the crime at about the time the murder was committed.

At that point the plea bargain comes into play. In our example, the district attorney may know that it will be difficult obtaining a guilty verdict from a jury on the murder charge. The public defender may also know that the jury will not let his client walk out of the courtroom a free man. As a minimum the defendant will be convicted on a robbery charge and his previous record will not play well with a jury. So the parties start their pow-wow.

The district attorney takes back the murder charge and the call for the death penalty and offers manslaughter and 25 years in prison. The defense offers violent robbery with accidental death and 10 years behind bars[44]. At the end they find common ground with manslaughter and involuntary death with 15 years in prison. The only thing missing now is convincing the defendant that the brokered deal is the best bargain he could get.

Because of the lack of alternatives and for fear, getting the death penalty in the end, the defendant signs his agreement to the negotiated deal. A plea bargain comes with the rule that the signed deal is legally bulletproof, meaning, it is almost impossible to challenge it in a higher court, does not include the possibility of early release or parole or asking for a re-trial if new evidence surmounts. So far; so good!

---

[44] Source: Pleas and Charge Bargaining, Bureau of Justice Assistance; U.S. Department of Justice.

But what if the defendant really did not shoot the person in the gas station but was the result of an unrelated tragedy that happened after the robbery? What if the defendant had little knowledge of the American justice system, who does anyway, and he was unaware of the consequences signing a plea bargain? ´Bad luck´ is what some hard lining citizens supporting a zero tolerance against all evil doers might say.

What may sound like an exceptional case is a fact on federal level. 98% of all federal cases are ´ruled´ by plea bargains. Why there are still federal courts you might ask? Probably the short staffed federal prosecutors are fully occupied with the remaining 2% and are happy about the relief.

It is easy to imagine that in a plea bargain the fate of a defendant depends a lot on the bargaining skills of the parties on the two sides of the gambling table. If, on one side, the district attorney is a professional poker player and on the other side, the public defender a rather inexperienced greenhorn, the defendant certainly has a bad hand in the game and he is not even holding the cards. This reminds me of one of the now-famous one-liners of Donald Rumsfeld during the second Iraq War; ´stuff happens´.

What would happen if all cases that are currently ´ruled´ through plea bargains would be handled in court, the place we thought it should be? Would it mean fairer trials, more justice or even lower sentences? None of the above.

Studies have revealed that in cases where the defendants really saw a court room, the average sentencing was tougher than through plea bargains, particularly if the defendant was black. It really appears that in most cases plea bargains are the better deal. A disturbing fact!

Movie Recommendations:
- *The Judge starring Robert Downey Jr.*

43. Out of Sight

H olding a world record, in most cases, is an honorable and great achievement. But there are world records which could easily make it into the Guinness Book of World Records but which are not suitable for fame and glory. This is particularly true to the incarceration rate in the United States.

There is no country on this planet, not even countries like China or North Korea, which both could easily be considered holding the ´top spot´, where there is a higher percentage of the population sitting behind bars than in the ´land of the free´. What an irony!

In 2012, 710 out of every 100,000 people in America spent their time in governmentally owned penal institutions. In comparison, the OECD average is 115 people. In Germany the number is 79[45]. In other words, the United States locks away six times more people than the international average[46].

How could that happen? Some major reasons were the drugs and gang criminality which had its grip on the United States during the 1980s.

---

[45] Source: OECD

[46] Source: The Hamilton Project: Ten Economic Facts about Crime and Incarceration in the United States, accessed on February 02, 2015

Some of the big cities had plenty of districts which were more or less 'no-go' areas. It was recommended to either bypass certain parts of a city or only enter it heavily armed. Even touristic places like Hollywood had its dark sides. If you parked your car just a few steps behind the Chinese Theater in one of the small alleys while marching along the Walk of Fame, it could had well been, that the car was heavily damaged or gone completely.

New, tough laws were used against the crime spree, like the 'Anti-Drug Abuse Act of 1986' or the known rule of 'Three Strikes and you are out', meaning three sentencings, regardless for what, were the free ticket for a lifelong accommodation with bed and breakfast paid by Uncle Sam.

The police and courts were able to clean the streets of criminal elements. Jails and prisons filled-up rapidly but were soon overcrowded. New penitentiaries were built, quite often managed by private corporations. Some of those privately run institutions even got guaranteed occupation rates written into their contracts. Who said justice, punishment and maximizing profits would not go well together?

Crime rates went straight south from the late 1980s until today. Some precincts in New York or Los Angeles, which were once known for gang activities and shootings where barely anyone walked the streets at night, are now hip parts of these cities. Nevertheless, the sentencing and incarceration rates remained historically high. On first sight it may appear that there is a connection between reduced crime rates and tough and harsh sentencing and punishment.

However, during the last 25 years crime rates also went down in the civilized world outside the United States without accompanying high incarceration rates. It became obvious that tough sentencing has little to do with the ups and downs of crime rates.

But there is a undisputable connection between high number of inmates and sky high incarceration costs. In the last 20 years the costs of the penal system has surged from USD 20 billion to more than USD 80 billion a year today[47].

The conclusion, that long prison sentences have little influence on crime and the difficulty to finance the high prison population, have led to a change of mind. Some states have lowered their ´Three Strikes and you are out´ laws and delinquents are sentenced to life in prison less often now in cases where only minor crimes were committed.

Movie Recommendations:
-   *Angels with Dirty Faces starring James Cagney*
-   *Escape from Alcatraz starring Clint Eastwood*

---

[47] Source: U.S. Census Bureau

44.   Hang´em High

There is still a majority in America today supporting the ultimate punishment, although the number of those opposing it is increasing slowly. Today, 18 U.S. states have abolished the death penalty, 32 states to go.

The United States are by far not the only country which regularly executes people. Other examples are popular destinations like Iran or North Korea. India, China and Saudi Arabia are also part of this illustrious list of countries. It may be a strange coincidence that most of the countries where the death penalty enjoys some popularity belong to the economic, political or military enemies of the United States. Better than having nothing in coming, some may think.

Reasons to re-consider the death penalty are plenty. The two most important are the numerous wrong sentencings and, hard to believe, the availability of killing instruments.

The number of innocent prisoners, some of them are awaiting their executions for decades while their cases go through all judicial steps, has increased rapidly during the last couple of years. The cases of these people were reopened because new witnesses came up, some witnesses revised their statements and, most importantly, DNA results proved the innocence of persons sentenced to death.

Of course the vast majority of people sitting on death row is undoubtedly guilty. But as long there is only one innocent person among the guilty ones, the death penalty system should be seriously questioned. It does not help the executed dead much if their innocence is only proven post mortem.

Executing people is an expensive business nowadays. Killing people legally is far from being a short exercise like we have seen in many Western movies. In those movie the defendants receive the death penalty in a court room, who looks as it is being used as a saloon at night, on a Sunday afternoon, right after church, another controversy among the faithful for which there are surely some fitting explanations in the Good Book, then the delinquent is put in jail overnight while the gallows are put together and is being hanged the following day as part of the county fair. May god have mercy with his swinging soul!

Today, it typically takes many, many years between the death sentencing of a defendant in court and the day of execution. The proceedings are not only time consuming but also very expensive. Depending on the state and the case it often costs up to a two-digit million amount just to execute a person. For that amount the person plus 4 or 5 more delinquents could easily be put behind bars for the rest of their natural life[48].

If the day has finally come, or it should be said came, the prisoner was put to death by lethal injection, served in 3 menus, one for euthanizing, one for paralyzing and one for killing. Of course the ingredients for that poisonous cocktail can't be bought in your local Walgreen's. In fact it is rather difficult obtaining these chemicals. Until a few years ago, these chemicals were mostly imported from European pharmaceutical companies.

As European chemical and pharma companies do not really want to read in the press that they are considered accessories to governmental or state sanctioned killing, these companies have stopped the supply of these lethal chemicals. This put the American execution system into serious, barely solvable problems, sometimes with fatal consequences.

There are unconfirmed rumors and unverified reports of break-ins in laboratories, even in prisons, where lethal chemicals required for the poison cocktail were stolen. In some cases the thieves might have come from other prisons where death sentences could no longer be executed due to the lack of supplies.

---

[48] Source: www.deathpenalty.org, accessed on June 03, 2015

Some states which don´t want to get behind their execution schedules have started referring to some old fashioned killing methods. Utah has started reactivating firing squads, moving from shooting needles to shooting bullets into the body of death row candidates.

Tennessee has taken the dust off their electric chairs, Arizona is soaking out the oxygen from their gas chambers while Oklahoma is experimenting with putting tight masks over the face of prisoners and choking them until their last breath has left their body. No matter what; the death show must go on while it still enjoys popular support.

Although little is being heard about it in the current election cycle; the numbers of executions are constantly going down[49]. In 1999, 98 people were killed in the name of justice; in 2015 ´only´ 35 out of the more than 3,000 people on death row were executed. In 2014 only seven U.S. states were still executing prisoners. Similar positive numbers also come from the court rooms. In 1994, 315 people were sentenced to death, while the number went down to 72 in 2014, the lowest number since 1974.

There are a few good reasons for that. There is the realization that the old propagated assumption that the death penalty has little to no impact on the rise or fall of crime rates, a conclusion most countries have made decades ago. Some things take a bit longer in the U.S.

---

[49] Source: Death Penalty Information Center: The Death Penalty Year End Report

Another issue is the proven innocence of death row candidates, often after they served decades in prison as already stated before. Then there are the horrifying reports of some cases from death cells where the ´humane´ executions by lethal injection took hours instead of minutes.

Movie Recommendations:
- *A good day for a Hanging starring Fred MacMurray*
- *One Way Passage starring William Powell*
- *Hang ´em high starring Clint Eastwood*

45.   Gun Fury

W hen we think about the over 300 million guns, where there is no register there can´t be an exact figure, and the regular reports from gun sales, we might get the impression that America would be nothing less than a big gun arsenal where every American would be armed to their teeth and a country constantly in a stage of war. No wonder Ted Cruz was calling for a 'War Time President', we instantly hope he was not referring to himself, although he might have meant something else with that one-liner during the primaries. But the world, even in a country that likes to reduce everything to black and white, is not that simple, not even in America.

In a recent survey, a good 1/3rd of Americans confirmed owning one or more guns[50]. 46% or the men and an astonishing 23% of the women claim to be gun owners. On the positive side, 51% of the Americans say that there is no gun in their home.

Gun ownership also seems to be a question of age, political affiliation and regional aspects are also to be considered. Gun enthusiasm seems to be strongest among those under 30 and those older than 60. Gun opponents are most common in the east. According to a NORC survey at the

---

Source: Gallup: Self Reported Gun Ownership, 2011, accessed on May 15, 2015.

University of Chicago it is twice as likely that there is a gun in households voting Republican as compared to Democratic[51]. 60% of Democrats say that they don´t have any guns at all, compared to 43% of Republicans[52].

Although the gun lobby and some media outlets would like to tell you otherwise, gun ownership in relation to the population has gone down during the last few decades, as more and more people moved from rural parts of the country, where a gun at home, particularly for hunting, is nothing special, to ever larger cities. On the same note, the guns in circulation have sky rocked. What do we make out of it? More and more guns are being held in less and less hands.

Besides that, or maybe because of it, the gun industry and political pundits save neither time nor money, lots of it, to implant the impression that owning a gun would be as is normal as owning a tooth brush and that there is no part if life which would not require a fully armed and trigger-ready population.

When you walk through a supermarket in the United States and pass the magazine stands, you might note the high number of gun magazines, particularly in relation to others subjects like travel, the economy or home improvement. These glossy papers offer something for every taste, regard-

---

[51] Source: Washington Post: Republicans are twice as likely as Democrats to live in a household with a gun, accessed on March 11, 2015

[52] Source: Gallup: Self Reported Gun Ownership, 2011, accessed on May 15, 2015

less how bad. There are publications for hand guns to be used at home, for hunting rifles to take out big game, machine guns and assault rifles to prepare against an attack by those out there...you know...terrorists, foreigners, Democrats, three huggers and other evil doers alike. Interestingly, those magazines almost exclusively cover white people. I am not sure whether anyone noticed or cared.

Those magazines once only catered to men. This has changed too and today there are some publications exclusively published for women. On the cover there are often women who are staged as brave housewives protecting their children with a smooth hand gun. Classic women role model and emancipation alike!

A study in 2001 revealed a strong connection between abonnements of magazines like Guns & Ammo and the sale of guns[53]. The more magazines are being sold, the more guns are acquired.

Every year, more than 30,000 people in America die through guns. Only less than half die through crime and homicides. Most die of suicides and by accidents in the safety of a home or while taking the family hunting.

---

[53] Source: Journal of Political Economy 2001: More Guns, More Crime, Mark Duggan / University of Chicago.

There is the grandfather who shoots his grandchildren while cleaning his gun. There is the little girl who coincidentally detects her father's gun in the night drawer and puts a hole through her brother's head.

There is the 6-year old girl in Sanford, FL who found the gun of her babysitter, took it, fired it and who shot herself. There is this story of an 11-year old boy in Tennessee who shot an 8-year old girl in the neighborhood with a 12-gauge shot gun because she did not let him see her puppies. The boy faces a first degree murder charge.

Cases like these which happen 50 times every single day, two every hour, but almost never raise any public attention. Most of those incidents do not make it into the news at all or are buried between two commercials and forgotten the next minute.

Obviously the daily roster of people shot in a crime or through tragic events raises less eyebrows than the latest nonsense from the Kardashian clan. This is what President Barack Obama meant when he said that the people got numb on gun related incidents and the dead have no voice.

The lack of public interest in the people dying through other people firing a gun makes any discussion reducing or minimizing this high annual number of victims more or less impossible. This includes even useful improvements like gun safety locks or 'smart' guns that can only be fired by its owner.

This does not mean that there are no concerned citizens, in fact there are a few million out there who would at least consider tougher gun laws, like mayors in communities, mothers, teachers and most importantly, law enforcement and crime investigation[54]. So there is hope out there. In Germany there is the saying that 'hope is the last to die' and certainly not through a gun shot.

Movie and TV Recommendations:
- *Gun Fury starring mit Rock Hudson*
- *Gun Glory starring Stewart Granger*
- *Gun Grazy starring Peggy Cummings*
- *Law and Order starring Ronald Reagan*

---

[54] Source: Everytown for Gun Safety

46.   The wild, Wild West...

The 2nd amendment to the U.S. Constitution, on which today´s interpretation of the right to a practically unlimited gun ownership is based, has its roots in the wake of the Revolutionary War when the then British government tried to disarm the colonial Americans to keep them at bay and to prevent armed uprisings.

The intention back then is the prime argument today to prevent any, really any considerations or steps towards less guns in the country or at least safer guns. Put aside what the Founding Fathers really had in mind when they phrased and worded the 2nd amendment at a time when guns were front loading pistols and muskets able to just firing one shot at a time followed by manually reloading powder and bullet before the gun could be fired again.

It can only be imagined what Thomas Jefferson, John Jay or Benjamin Franklin might have done differently would they had foreseen that one day a Supreme Court decisions would allow its citizens stockpiling semi-automated machine guns and assault rifles which can fire 1,000 or more rounds a minute.

The authors of the 2nd amendments, passed on December 15, 1791, probably had little ideas of today´s urbanization with millions of people living in ever bigger cities. They wrote the constitution and its amendments at a time when the vast majority of the American citizens lived in the wilderness where dangers were still plenty and hunting essential.

Today´s gun enthusiasts also like to refer to the good old frontier days, where law abiding citizens marched out of Sunday church directly in the saloon next door with the gun belt holstered and always ready and prepared to draw their colts in the cause of the slightest danger. Those who believe that have certainly read too much pulp western or seen too many B-Western movies. Reality was far from that.

Americans back then, regardless whether in an east coast brick mansion or in wooden shags in the west, going shopping in Boston or joining a weekend dance in Cheyenne, saw no reason walking around in public carrying guns. Always carrying a Winchester, a Springfield rifle or even a Colt Single Action Army would have felt like weight lifting. Constantly carrying a sidearm probably would cause hip problems over time. But most importantly, carrying guns within city limits was widely spread prohibited and forbidden.

Owning guns was common among the rural population in the 18th and 19th century, no doubt. Guns were essential for hunting and protection from wolves and bears. In rare cases, a lot rarer than in Western movies, novels and even some history books may tell, guns were also needed fighting off marauding bandits and Indians on war path.

What is barely being told or discussed how the brave citizens and lawmen in the good ole west in the years after the Civil War, at a time when Colt and Winchester became the popular guns of the time, ensured peace in their communities and kept any kind of gunplay at a minimum and rare occasion.

The American people back then, especially in the so-called Wild West, realized how important it is to protect their women, children and, most importantly, each other from too many guns in public places and the inevitable violence that comes with it. This was particularly true in the wildest of all cities and towns of the west, like Deadwood, Dodge City or Tombstone.

As early as 1813, states like Kentucky or Arkansas had forbidden carrying concealed guns. Between 1880 and 1915 many states and most of the cities and communities passed laws, rules and regulations on who could wear guns when and where[55].

In Tombstone, Arizona, the town near Tucson, where one of the most famous gun fights between two enemy parties played out at the OK Corral, on one side the Earp brothers and Doc Holiday and on the other side the Clantons and McLaurys. This incident, captured in so many movies and TV shows overshadows another fact about this western town. In the

---

[55] Source: Franklin Zimring and Gordon Hawkins: The citizens guide to gun control, 1987

1880s it was not allowed to carry guns within city limits[56]. Did you know that the OK Corral was outside city limits?

In the 1870s, Wichita, Kansas posted signs at the town borders requested all people to deposit their guns at the police headquarter where they got a token with a number on it. They got back their guns on their way out of town by returning the token.

Other towns required gun and belts to be stored in a stable, saloon or the sheriff´s office while in town. Many had public signs informing visitors where to deposit their guns. Some of these signs had very clears messages like the one used in the movie ´Western Cyclone´ from 1943 starring Buster Crabbe where a sign in the local saloon said that ´Hang your hardware here and you won´t be hung yourself´.

Similar strict regulations were known to infamous western towns like Deadwood or Dodge quite opposite the picture provided in Western movies and novels creating a history that never was. [57]

The people at their time back then surely had the same respect for the 2nd amendment to the Constitution. But they obviously had a more unbiased look at the Constitution and made use of the flexibility it offers, the way a lot of other aspects of the Constitution are being handled.

---

[56] Source: Politico: Even Tombstone had gun laws, January 10 2011, accessed on July 08, 2015

[57] Source: Huffington Post: Adam Winkler: Gunfight – The Battle to Bear Arms in America, accessed on July 11, 2015

Why is it so difficult today, even for the Supreme Court? Is there really no room to allow for clear rules regarding the carrying and maintaining of guns for the better and the safety of the society in the interpretation of the Constitution without jeopardizing the general right to own a gun. Maybe a look back into history would help. Good luck with that.

Even the conservative voice on the Supreme Court, the late Antonin Scalia pointed out in the case of 'the United States vs. Heller' that the Second Amendment is not unlimited and leaves room for regulations[58].

Movie Recommendations:
- *Support your local Sheriff starring James Garner*
- *Wichita starring Joel McCrea*
- *The hour of the Gun starring James Garner*
- *Gunfight at OK Corral starring Kirk Douglas*
- *Frontier Marshal starring Randolph Scott*

---

[58] Source: Bret Baier, Fox News, Republican Presidential Debate

47. The Carry Show

Nowadays many U.S. states allow carrying guns in the open as it would be sunglasses. It is called ´Open Carry´ and is one of the main initiatives of the gun lobby keeping courts and politicians busy. In general a frightening development which has reached a level of craziness not seen anywhere else on this planet and never before in history, especially not in the U.S. history. You do not have to be a pacifist to be scared being surrounded by people carrying their weapons around in public. I even had my own share of strange encounters with the armed and dangerous.

A few years ago while on a roundtrip through the west my wife and I unloaded our car and moved into a motel room for the night, somewhere in Wyoming. At that moment a ´hunting party´ moved in next door. Three hunters in camouflage were loaded with guns ready for WW III. In reality they probably just hunted a few rabbits or wild hogs.

All of us who at least have once spent a night in a roadside motel know that the walls are so thin that you can hear the TV commercials 3 rooms away. You can imagine how we felt spending the night next to this group of guys hoping they would not be too drunk or would not be smoking too much of the wrong stuff before fantasizing about big game hunting and starting shooting off their guns. We really felt relieved next morning and the guys next door where smiling at us before heading for breakfast. But even then we wondered if those hunting rifles would not had been better stored in a locked place instead of leaning against the bed.

In 2013 my wife and I were joining the festivities of the Arizona centennial celebration in Prescott, the first capital of Arizona. On our way from our parking lot to city hall an old guy crossed the street in front of us holstering a semi-automated pistol open-carry, visible for everyone. At that moment a thousand thoughts crossed my mind. Is he still healthy? Is his mind still clear? Is he a nervous old fellow who might pull the gun in a stressful situation? Of course, nothing happened and the old guy probably would have wondered about my thoughts if he could have read them.

These examples are brief, harmless encounters with open carry gun laws as they only exist in the United States. In no other country on the western hemisphere is there a country were a fraction of today´s population considers it a good idea carrying around loaded guns like a pet. Today, Open Carry is allowed in a majority of U.S. states, sometimes requiring a permit, sometimes even without it. The year 2016 started with a celebration in Texas, where the Governor proudly signed into law Open Carry in the Lone Star State.

Besides Open Carry, there are Concealed Weapon regulations, ensuring that plenty of guns are in circulation and people are being shot to death. Cynics might say why producing these millions of guns if nobody would use it. Every additional gun on the street is a boost for the economy. There are states were carrying concealed guns is allowed as alternative Open Carry rules. There are also states where only concealed weapons are allowed[59].

Between 1977 and 1998 23 U.S. states enacted Concealed Weapon laws; today it is possible in all states. You should expect that every day a few million people in the United States are walking around holstering guns. You might be surprised how often you were sitting in a coffee shop or a diner and the person sitting on the table in the next booths hides a semi-automatic pistol under his sweater. The right to carry concealed weapons sometimes triggers strange developments. Take that restaurant owner in Indianapolis who gives a 25% discount to customers carrying a concealed weapon license.[60]Gail Collins stated in her column in the New York Times that ´in most states you can get a license to carry a concealed weapon without demonstrating that you know how to fire it. In the other states, the bar is generally still below sea level´.

Movie Recommendations:
- *Falling Down starring Michael Douglas*
- *The Wild Bunch starring William Holden*

---

[59] Source: Lives Saved or Lives Lost? The Effects of Concealed-Handgun Laws on Crime, Hashem Dezhbakhsh and Paul H. Rubin in The American Economic Review, Vol. 88. May 1998, accessed on May 15, 2015

[60] Source: USA Today, October 29, 2015

48. Tension in the class room

The most extreme and loudest supporters of unlimited gun ownership, handling and ultimately firing don´t stop short anywhere in their relentless efforts getting rid of the remaining places of gun control. This includes places where kids and students should learn anything but playing and tossing around with guns. For many years there are attempts by the gun lobby to allow students and teachers to carry guns, open or concealed, on campus of universities and colleges.

After every shootings at colleges or universities and even before the gun smoke has faded away and the victims are buried, the gun proponents are crawling out of the holes and claiming that such tragedies could be prevented if the teachers, and even the students, were armed. In cases of an attack the armed electorate and student body would put their guns out of their rucksacks and spray a full load of bullets into any assailant.

Students, or almost any other ordinary person who never were involved in a lethal situation, cannot be expected to react calmly and focused when under stress created by an unexpected incident. If they are armed, do we really believe students would show no nerves like Clint Eastwood or Charles Bronson, or would they rather be under a lot of stress and their good intentions would end in an even bloodier carnage if the boys and girls would start emptying their guns? Would students with little or no shooting experience be able to really target an attacker or would their shaking hands rather kill their fellow class-mates? Would students and their teachers, who might have never shot at anything but some deer while hunting or who only did some target practicing using empty cans be able killing another person with a gun, regardless how dangerous this person might be?

I served in the army and I know how to handle a gun. Not only that, I know how difficult it is to precisely hit a target. Anyone who spent time in the armed forces will tell you how much and ongoing practice it takes to maintain a steady hand and aim when firing a gun. Speaking of the military; carrying around guns on military compounds and facilities while not practicing is unheard of. The armed forces have procedures to ensure that soldier don´t walk around armed while off-duty.

Ask any police officer how much training it took before they were first allowed to carry a gun. Psychological training also is an important layer and mandatory component of the education in law enforcement before a police officer is allowed patrolling his or her beat strapping a gun. New York police commissioner Bill Bratton told New York Times columnist Gail Collins ´Police on average, for every 10 rounds fired…actually strike something once or twice, and they are highly trained´. What would the results be for all the untrained gun owners? What, or, even more importantly, whom would they hit while trying the intended target?

But on campus all these precautions seem to be obsolete, no matter how physically and mentally stable an armed student may be. It is easy to imagine what might happen in class room, if a psychological instable student unsatisfied with his latest test results or in a rivalry with a fellow student is pulling a gun to seek revenge or just to make his point. Add alcohol or drugs to the equation and you don´t even need an outside attacker to create a massacre.

Thanks to millions of concerned parents, teachers, police officers, mayors and other public officials a portion of these attempts have failed so far. But quite too many succeed.

Texas is the ninth U.S. state where students are allowed to carry concealed guns on campus of public schools[61]. The only requirement is a formless request and a minimum age of 21 years, meaning that at the same time a student is allowed to legally buy alcohol, they are also allowed to carry around guns. If you have kids and want them to receive a college or university degree in the United States you might want to check out the school very carefully. Otherwise is could happen, that your kid ends up in a class full of armed students.

Even places of worship aren´t safe places anymore. Some pastors bring guns into the pulpit always ready on the draw while holding the Good

---

[61] Source: USA Today, June 10, 2015: Texas prepares to join the college-carry craze

Book in the other hand.[62] Tennessee Lt. Governor Ron Ramsey, Republican, of course, told his fellow citizens that Christians ˊserious about their faithˊ should think about getting guns.

Movie Recommendations:
- *Crime School starring Humphrey Bogart*
- *Blackboard Jungle starring Glenn Ford*
- *Murder on the Blackboard starring Edna May Oliver*
- *Kindergarten Cop starring Arnold Schwarzenegger*

---

[62] Source: Rob Schenck on guns, Time, October 12, 2015

49.   Shoot first; ask later

Individual freedom and happiness are high values which need to be cherished and protected. Nobody will doubt that it is the right of each individual to self-defend and fight for these rights, particularly in the case of physical danger. It gets a bit tricky though if it is not even certain yet, that there is a clear and present danger out there but nevertheless applying self-defending measures. Let us take an example to illustrate that.

Let us imagine a person unknown to you on first sight is crossing the street in front of your home in long curves and is short-cutting his way through your lawn to get to the house on the bordering parcel and you would fear for your home, family and life, maybe not in that particular order. You take your revolver out of your night drawer, walk outside and empty the gun on the person drifting through your property.

After you got a hold on your senses again and you are switching on the lights in your garden, you realize that the dead body lying on the lawn is your dear neighbor returning from an evening of intense boozing and gambling. Later on, after the police has arrived and starts asking questions you refer to some local laws and claim having acted in self-defense. If law enforcement and the court confirm your claims and are setting you free, you are most likely living in a state were a 'Stay Your Ground' law applies.

Since 2000, Stay Your Ground laws, sometimes also referred to as 'Castle Doctrine', were enacted in more than 20 U.S. states with differing levels of flexibility under which conditions you can shoot someone and claiming self-defense afterwards.

There are a few interesting findings in the states were Stay Your Ground has become the law of the land. Let us take Florida as an illustration. It turned out that almost all people in the state who shot other humans and claimed self-defense based on the Stay Your Ground law had a criminal record or were otherwise known to the police.

On federal level it turned out that in states were Stay Your Ground laws were enacted gun inflicted deaths followed by self-defense claims soared 85% although the overall number of violent deaths has decreased significantly[63]. In other words there are fewer and fewer homicides and deadly manslaughters overshadowed by a high number of people shot just because there is a law allowing people to shoot others without being held responsible for it.

---

[63] Source: Tampa Bay News

The supporters of Stay Your Ground laws claim that these initiatives increase the safety on the streets and on private property. That the reality is quite different is no surprise, at least on this side of the Atlantic.

The Texas A&M University has browsed through FBI files of the last 10 years and unearthed evidence showing that Stay Your Ground laws did not improve the number of robberies, break-ins or violence[64].

What the study found out instead is, that the number of deaths by guns shot up by 8% which relates to 600 dead people per state where Stay Your Ground was introduced into law. A study of the National Bureau of Economic Research reached similar conclusions.

If it so obvious that a free pass to shoot around not only has little to no impact on the prevention of crime but also rather increases the number of deaths in the name of self-defense, why does it not create an outcry in the population and a change of mind. Are the numbers and the negative impacts of Stay Your Ground not known or ignored? Is the gun lobby really so strong? Does a society want to tolerate that on the long run? We will see.

---

[64] Source: Does Strengthening Self-Defense Law Deter Crime or Escalate Violence, Cheng Cheng and Mark Hoekstra.

As so often, there is a positive edge to it. In at least 10 states, including Florida, Stay Your Ground laws were modified and scaled back so that not every person shot in the neighborhood can be claimed as self-defense.

On the disturbing and negative side it needs to be mentioned that 13 other states have even further liberated their local Stay Your Ground. Sometimes you win, sometimes you lose and sometimes you lose your life because of strange, some might say stupid, laws.

Movie Recommendations:
- *Draw starring Kirk Douglas*
- *Gun the man down starring Angie Dickinson*
- *The quick gun starring Audie Murphy*
- *The gun hawk starring Rory Calhoun*

50.   Gun Reciprocity

T he never tiring gun lobby spends a lot of money and effort to circumvent or even nullify gun laws in those states which still dare regulating gun acquisition and ownership. The money comes from the full war chest of the lobby collected from its members and supporters. The effort is provided by politicians with ambitions.

In a strange twist of attitude the gun lobby is attacking gun laws on state levels. Where the sovereignty of the individual states is normally highly protected, it all of a sudden becomes obsolete if it could result in gun controlling laws to be weakened.

One of the latest assaults on public order and common sense is the initiative to introduce reciprocity on gun laws. This, if enacted, would mean that gun laws applicable to a gun owner in one state should be equally valid in any state a proud gun owner is visiting. The ´Constitutional Concealed Carry Reciprocity Act of 2014´ introduced into the Senate (S. 1908) would foresee that the most liberal of all gun laws would prevail over more conservative gun control laws. How would that play out in practice? Let us take a few examples for illustration.

People with certain criminal records are prohibited from buying guns from registered gun traders. Gun shops are required to perform background checks to ensure a potential buyer does not have such criminal records. However, Arizona has a flourishing business with unregistered gun traders offering their deadly merchandise in gun shows like home-made pies on a flea market. In addition there are countless online websites where guns can be bought, sold and traded unregulated.

If someone with a criminal record would be able to legally acquire a gun at a public gun show in Arizona, the proposed law would allow this person to also legally own this gun in other states. A study revealed that in 1 of 30 gun trades transacted online, people prohibited from owning guns could easily buy one at a gun selling website.

Today, all 50 states and the District of Columbia have enacted some sort of Concealed Weapon laws but in 5 states, among them Arizona and Wyoming, a permit to acquire a gun is not required. Under the proposed law a person who bought a gun in Wyoming without a permit could carry the gun in another state where a permit is required.

In Colorado, a person who is requesting a Concealed Weapon permit has to be at least 21 years old and has to undergo mandatory gun practice training. In Washington State, gun trainings are also required, but performing the training online is sufficient[65].

---

[65] Source: Everytown for Gun Safety

What the United States have in common with most countries is the fact that laws almost never leave Congress the way they entered it. Some law initiatives were buried before they saw the light of day. The gun reciprocity law seems to go down that path; at least it did go nowhere in 2014. But the sponsor of this controversial bill, Senator John Cornyn of Texas does not seem to give up that easily. He tried it again in 2015 with bill S. 498. The latest bets that this law would be passed are set at 1%[66].

---

[66] Source: www.govtrack.us/congress/bills/114/s498

51. Gun Sanity

After each gun incident in America people around the globe are wondering what is wrong with the United States. The former mayor of New York, Michael Bloomberg once said after another mass shooting at a school ´only we got this problem´. But what exactly is the problem? Is there a deeply rooted aggressiveness and violent tendency that leads to so much trigger happiness and constantly high numbers of people shot every year? Probably not!

Is it the gun lobby and certain right-leaning media which created the illusion of a scared and unprotected population whose safety can only reclaimed and guaranteed by an arsenal of guns? I let that hang in there. During the same time, almost no safety measures were introduced preventing people shooting themselves accidentally. Quite the opposite; even the smallest attempts regarding gun safety measures are being attacked by the gun lobby and conservative politicians are too scared to touch anything which could be labeled gun control. During the presidency of George W. Bush Congress enacted a law preventing law enforcement from keeping track and publishing information where criminals got a hold on guns.[67]

---

[67] Source: The New York Times, December 30, 2015

How do other countries react in case of gun violence? What countries like England, Australia or even Switzerland have in common is, that after tragic gun incidents the people in public and in politics analyze how such incident could be prevented in future whereas some parties in America brushing the reasons away with typical slogans like ´Now it is not the time to talk about gun control´. Unfortunately these voices never let it known, when it would be a good time to address it.

Where other countries strengthening their laws and regulations to acquire and own guns the American gun lobby wants to even further arm the population. Some smart and tough gun laws in the United Kingdom ensure that almost nobody on the British islands is allowed to own hand guns. It should be no big surprise to hear that the UK almost never has to mourn people shot to death. Just across the border in Canada gun restrictions on hand guns and automatic weapons goes back to 1930. After a mass killing in 1989 restrictions also applied to rifles and shotguns. Today, almost all types of guns have to be registered and every gun owner needs a license although gun ownership is as popular part of the tradition in rural Canada as south of the border[68].

What would need to happen for the United States to realize that only less guns floating around and stronger gun control rules are the only way

---

[68] Source: New York Times, October 15, 2015

to reduce the number of people dying by bullets? Maybe it takes a miracle. Until that happens, the dead will keep piling up. RIP.

There is a strange aspect in the gun battle. The gun lobby and literally all Republican candidates for the presidency constantly hold up the 2nd amendment to bear arms. But even they have limits to their demands. Have you ever heard the gun lobby supporting the ownership of nukes or rocket launchers? These are arms too! Why do they fight for the right of Americans be allowed to own an AK 47 but not a Stinger rocket? Have you ever heard the gun lobby requiring that it should be allowed taking guns on a plane? Why should it not be possible to carry-on an AK 47 on a commercial flight?

Because it just might open many eyes and maybe many more would start asking themselves serious questions. Because it quickly becomes obvious that there are and must indeed be limits and rules to the right to bear arms. This is a conclusion probably in line with the silent majority of gun owners.

In 2015 more people in America were killed by guns than by automobiles. While gun deaths remain at a constantly high level, there had been equally constant declines in deaths by car accidents year over year. The difference is obvious. To reduce the number of people dying in traffic, anti-lock brakes, seat belts, airbags, electronic stability systems, sensors to signal a driver drifting off the shoulder, rear view cameras or automatic speed reducing speed or stopping a car if getting too close to the car up front, to just name a few, were developed and, quite often, enforced by law during the last decades.

It might not be too long until gun deaths will surpass drug deaths, although that number is still a lot higher. 2014 47,000 died through drugs. Interestingly the highest portions of drug deaths are white men in their late 40s and 50s. White men in this age groups are also the biggest supporters of gun rights as well as the highest percentage of Americans ending their life with a gun.

The sum of all these non-natural deaths have caused the mortality in that age group to rise in stark contrast to almost all other countries worldwide. While the mortality rate in the age group between 45 and 55 was 400 out of 100,000 Americans and Canadians in 1990, the figures are now 470 in America and 280 in Canada. The difference is almost solely blamed on drug overdoses and gun suicides. Some cynics call it the dark side of American exceptionalism[69].

On January 7, 2016 CNN hosted a town hall forum for President Obama where he discussed the gun issue with supporters of stricter gun control and opposition to any kind of interference with the 2nd amendment, gun owners, gun sellers and those who have never owned a gun, like President Obama.

---

[69] Source: Center for Disease Control and Prevention/Handelsblatt/PNAS, January 22, 2016

CNN anchor Anderson Cooper opened the event referring to the 30,000 something gun deaths a year and that $2/3^{rd}$ are suicides and accidents. This unbelievable high number year after year is disturbing enough and it is strange that a country, at least those voices that are being heard, seems accepting this as an OK status. One person in the audience of the George Mason University in Fairfax, Virginia countered ´why not celebrate where we are´, as if 30,000 dead people would offer some grounds for celebration.

There is a deeply rooted fear among many Americans, most of them voting Republican, that ´the Government´ intends taking away their guns. It seems that some people not only distrust their own elected officials but also their own Constitution. Considering that the 2nd amendment to bear guns has been re-confirmed many times by the Supreme Court and any event to change the constitution would require a $2/3^{rd}$ majority in both chambers of Congress plus the President. With a Congress that for many years could barely make up its mind on regular business like funding the Farm Bill or the annual budget and a country deeply divided on the issue there is no way that any initiative limiting gun ownership would make it into the Constitution or would alter the 2nd amendment in any foreseeable time.

The conspiracy fears also bear strange fruits. The President told the story of a regular military exercise in Texas where some folks seriously seemed to believe that the Government would start imposing martial law and taking over their town. I am not sure what TV stations these people watch, to what talk radio station they listen or which blogs they read but it must be media out of this world.

One of the participants in the audience also tried to explain how difficult it might be, even in the worst of intentions, taking away more than 300 million guns from about 65 million households. The discussion also offered possible actions that could be taken making the live of Americans safer, from the way guns are acquired, maintained and used. Let us start with the acquisition. According to recent surveys, 80% of the population is supporting some level of gun control. Gun control, first and foremost means making sure that only those eligible owning a gun are allowed buying one and that there are some prerequisites before a person is allowed firing a gun, for whatever purposes.

Only few states require at least some level of target practicing before buying a gun. We already talked about how difficult it is to fire a gun in a dire situation.

Next on the list would be registration of guns, both ways, the gun itself, those holding it, the manufacturers and traders straight through the list of all owners. Every gun, basically all its parts should have a registration number maintained by the manufacturer and could be checked by the authorities if the gun is involved in a crime. Once the manufactured gun leaves the plant all parties holding and owning it should be listed in a register equally accessible by the Police, FBI and other authorities, again only in the case of an investigation. This register could be maintained by a NGO or a governmental agency under strict data protection rules.

In case there would be a crime where a gun had been confiscated from a criminal, law enforcement could check the register and trying to find out how the gun could end up in a crime. This would also provide insights how guns are changing hands, legally and illegally, until they finally end up in the hands of a criminal.

In the town hall meeting a person in the audience said ´why can´t we title guns just like cars? ´He further concluded that if a car is transferred without title and the car is involved in an accident ´it´s on me´. In other words, if every gun would be registered, it could always be traced back to the last (legal) owner and law enforcement could find out how a gun could get into illegal hands and take preventive measures.

Whenever someone proposes that if there were less guns in the country, most guns would be in the hands of criminals. Well again, the UK and Australia did just that; drastically reducing the type of guns that are available for sale, most importantly prohibiting any type of semi-automatics. And you know what; gun violence and gun deaths went down to almost zero today.

Of course not every case of a gun possessed illegally involved in crimes can be prevented but reducing the likeliness of even saving a single live would be worth it. How can the high number of accidental gun deaths be reduced? So-called smart guns would be solution where a technology ensures that only the rightful owner can use it. Sounds liberal? Well, the proposal came from the CEO of Colt in 1997 as President Obama told the town hall folks and the millions at home. Smith & Wesson proposed the same under heavy attack by the NRA. Gun shops owners who wanted to sell smart guns received death threats.

How can the number of guns in the hand of criminals be reduced? Some people are on a no-fly list, almost everyone for a pretty good reason. But strange enough some circles have no problems allowing these people to buy and own guns.

Movie Recommendations:
- *A mad, mad, mad world starring Spencer Tracy*

Part VI

Evolution, Economy and Ecology

52.   Intelligent Curriculum

During the last centuries America had the opportunity to learn a lot about its history. Scientists have discovered that a comet which hit today´s Gulf of Mexico some 65 Million years ago caused the dinosaurs to extinct in the aftermath.

In large parts of the United States, particularly in the South West, for example in the Grand Canyon, fossils are being found up to this day allowing to ever better and more accurately piecing together the puzzle of the evolution from the Megafauna to today´s animals and plants.

Cave findings in New Mexico, like the Clovis arrows, tell the history from the migration of the natives arriving from Asia, crossing the Bering Street and arriving in today´s North and South America some 6,000 years ago.

Some believe it may have happened as early as 12,000 years ago or in several waves. At least this is the current status of science and written in most American schoolbooks, although Anthropology and Biology do not seem to be the favorite classes these days.

The general population and school districts still believe that students should learn about the history of earth based on scientific research. However, in many states there are religious and conservative circles tirelessly trying to undermine the curriculum in biology, geology and even history. They want to achieve that scientific facts should co-exist with questionable theories. Some want to ban certain facts completely from the class room.

The latest political attempts to ´enrich´ the natural sciences curriculum, not to say replacing it, with ´intelligent design´ occurred 2015 in the state congresses of Indiana (SB 562), Missouri (HB 486), Oklahoma (SB 665) and Montana (LC 1324).

In the opinion of the legislative initiative in Montana it said that teachers were insecure how to explain certain aspects and uncertainties of biology and geology to their flock in the classroom. Some might think text books and truckloads of scientific texts, books and reports should be able supplying the teachers with the necessary background and information.

But instead the teachers should be allowed to pinpoint the weaknesses of some scientific conclusions. If such initiatives would become law, it would be up to the teachers to decide which scientific research, findings and facts should be lectured as facts, questioned as unproven theories or even completely ignored.

An infamous conclusion from Donald Rumsfeld comes to mind. We may remember back when he dug through half of Iraq but still no weapons of mass destructions could be found anywhere. When presented with the facts, he concluded: ´The Absence of Evidence is not the Evidence of Absence´ in the sense of ´We did not find anything but something could had been there´.

Movie Recommendations:
- *Jurassic Park starring Jeff Goldblum*
- *Against all odds starring Richard Widmark*

53. Eternal Youth

How old is our dear blue planet we are inhibiting? Well, it is probably too early to provide an exact final figure while there are still so many open questions about the evolution of the universe and the earth in particular. Latest estimates for the universe stand at 13.8 billion years whereas the scientifically proven age of the earth is 4.8 billion years.

These incredible high numbers of years seem to be too much to swallow for many conservative Americans. Religious scripture does not provide any indication about the age of the earth but a few billion years seem to be pretty far-fetched, particularly at a time two thousand years ago where almost nobody could read and write or count to a billion. So what number to offer to today's faithful that might be more in line with the literal interpretation of the Good Book? How does 6,000 years sound?

The 6,000 years is circulating among certain conservatives for quite some time now. According to that, the earth is obviously not only very young, our planet does not age either. How come? Well, someone who claimed the earth is 6000 years old some 30 years ago, should he today not say 6,030 years? I let that thought swinging in there.

A part of the American population, also known as ´Young Earth Crea-tionists´, strongly supports the idea that a higher power created the world in roughly 6 days, exact working hours are not known, some 6,000 years ago. The number of supporters of that theory is nowhere higher than in the United States although the number differs strongly depending on the ques-tioning.

In a Gallup survey of 2012 46% of Americans said that the world was created less than 10,000 years by divine powers. This number is almost unchanged since the 1980s when Gallup started asking this question. However, if a similar question is being asked without reference to faith, only 25% claim the world being less than 10,000 years. It should be noted that both questions were asked in the same survey, so respondents provid-ed contradicting responses in the same questionnaire.

Whenever some fossils of dinosaurs are being found in America, which happens quite often, remember the comet, reports come up by sup-porters of the ´6,000-year-theory´ where they try to ´proof´ that humans and dinosaurs once peacefully lived together at the same time, at least during the time before the big flood, whenever that was.

A few years ago a footprint of a human was found in the fossil footstep of a dinosaur. For some this was a clear thing; an early human being was walking his Brontosaurus.

America also offers some exhibition halls, so-called 'museums', where the evolution story is shown with a lot of technical tricks and computer animated figures, like in Disney Land but without Donald Duck. Here too, humans are shown alongside dinosaurs.

The story goes that, rather than being extinct some 65 million years ago, after that huge comet hit the blue planet, the big beast did not make it onto the big boat a little while ago so they drowned and that is the last we saw from them, until Jurassic Park opened that is. On the positive side it has to be mentioned that there are less and less annual visitors to these strange venues. Maybe these places are also doomed to extinct. Evolution is merciless.

It is astonishing how easy it seems to be for some, ignoring and brushing away hundreds of years of scientific research and information gathering in anthropology, biology, geology and paleontology.

Almost every U.S. state now and then has to battle off intends by some groups who intend to insert evolution into science class. They want to achieve that schools would have to teach evolution or 'intelligent design' as a possible theory alongside others, like scientific research.

Thanks to millions of teachers, scientist and, most importantly, concerned parents there was little success so far to reduce the history of the world from a couple of billion years down to a few thousand.

President Woodrow Wilson too, was confronted with the pressing question about the age of the earth and the natural selection. He responded that, like any intelligent and educated person he is convinced about organic evolution. He was pretty surprised to hear that such a question is still being asked,

Movie Recommendations:
-   *Inherit the Wind starring Spencer Tracy*
-   *Religious starring Bill Maher*

54.   Stories of 1001 Nights

History has the tendency to be formed by those telling it. It is not always easy for story tellers keeping the facts together, especially if the original story and facts do not appeal to everyone in the audience or do not fit into the mindset and beliefs of those presenting it. Recent examples are at display in some former states of the Confederacy, where revisionism of historic events is taking place. In some history text books the slavery is no longer seen as the major reason but a rather minor aspect for the secession of the southern states and the subsequent Civil War. Instead it is stipulated that the fight between the blue and the grey was caused by the cultural differences deriving from the industrial progress in the north on one side and the traditional agriculture in the south on the other.

Some want to turn the civil rights movement and the demonstrations of the Black population of the 1960s into some sort of early terrorism, triggered and lead by members of the Black Panthers, the strong arm of an otherwise peaceful movement. This would play down the necessary changes and improvements the social turmoil brought to the Black people in the United States at a time when Blacks were still considered 2nd class by vast parts of the population and had to sit in the back of the bus. Some schools, particularly in the South, have already stopped teaching the dim reality about the late 1960s, like the fact that back then 80% of the population were against any type of relationship between Blacks and Whites.

In Texas there are text books in circulation which want to make students believe that the 10 Commandments and Moses, an early democratic, more likely a Republican, had inspired the Founding Fathers writing the U.S. Constitution although the exact opposite was the case. It was the freedom of Religion and the clear separation of state and church which built the pillars of the Constitution[70]. Furthermore, the Founding Fathers were rather catering to science. While the Declaration of Independence was adopted on July 4, 1776, Thomas Jefferson was working on a research project and recorded local temperatures. It is also no secret that Benjamin Franklin was a friend and supporter of science who experimented with electricity and lightning.[71]

Some text books are referring to slaves shipped from Africa under horribly conditions as bringing 'workers' to the United States. It makes the slave trade business look like as it was a win-win situation for all, the plantations which needed the human capital, the human traffickers shipping across the Atlantic selling the 'merchandise' and the slaves themselves who got great job opportunities picking cotton. If this would be lectured in school it would not take long if people would start believing that slavery was not that bad at all and Americans would need to longer

---

[70] Source: USA Today, November 14, 2014, Texas textbooks under a swirl of controversy

[71] Source: Newsweek, August 21, 2015

deal with a history of human trade, chaining, whipping, torturing and rap-
ing black people during the dark age of the young American nation.

Playing down the slavery in the South comes at a time when research
unearthed some disturbing facts from this cruel era. For a long time it was
thought, and lectured, that the South was opposed to industrialization and
progressive working methods when the Civil War began. Today it becomes evident that quite the opposite was the case, in a horrible way
though. It is believed that the slave owners used sophisticated measures to
improve the productivity of their slaves. They set clear, measureable goals
for their slaves. Violence and torture were used for motivation; those who
did not achieve the set production goals, be it plowing a field, picking or
cleaning cotton, were severely punished. That was another reason why
slaves were way more productive than free men which made the slaves
valuable assets. It is estimated that during the 1850s the value of the
American slaves was USD 1.3 billion or 20% of the public American
wealth. Some studies further conclude that the industrial revolution in the
United States would not had been possible without the slaves or that it
would had least been turned out differently without the millions of human
labor who were not paid, had not health coverage and no pension fund[72].

Movie Recommendations:
- *Good Will Hunting starring Matt Damon*
- *Storm warning starring Ronald Reagan*

---

[72] Source: Süddeutsche Zeitung, July 26, 2015

55. Plastic dreams on Hawaii

T he United States occupy the top spots among environmental sinners. The general population has little interest in protecting the environment. Climate change is considered by many as an invention by Democrats, liberal scientists and ´the media´ and all supporting studies and research are unproven theories at best.

But there are a few green islands amidst the grey reality. In 2014, the Hawaiian island banned plastic bags from shops and supermarkets. It might have been difficult in the beginning but it has become a success story, although visitors from the mainland might undergo a cultural choc when they can´t bag their groceries in a ton of plastic bags but have to buy a recyclable and reusable bag. There goes the unlimited freedom.

There are estimates by the oceanic organization Oceana that every single hour (!) some 300 tons of plastic waste end up in the oceans. A mountain of waste the oceans have to take in every year. A portion of that, about 3 tons have built a large plastic island circulating about 2,000 square kilometers north of Hawaii[73].

---

[73] Source: Der Spiegel, February 02, 2008, accessed on Spiegel Online July 10, 2015

There is the story about a wrecked ship with a container of 30,000 plastic toys which ended up in the ocean in 1992 which stranded on the beaches all over the coastal United States to this very day. No plastic animals were reported ashore Hawaii yet but it would be no surprise if someone would step into one while strolling on Waikiki Beach.

A bit away from Hawaii a group of islands and several atolls spreading over 12,000 square kilometers, a size as large as Germany was declared a natural preserve by the Bush administration where commercial shipping and fishing is prohibited. Who said George W. Bush would not be full of surprises. At least it was a very nice gesture at the end of his term which puts him in a much better light compared to some of stuff he authorized during the dark age of his presidency[74].

Movie and TV Recommendations:
- *Blue Hawaii starring Elvis Presley*
- *Pearl starring Angie Dickinson*
- *Pearl Harbor starring Ben Affleck*

---

[74] Source: Focus Online, June 17, 2006, accessed on July 10, 2015

56.   A place in the sun

One of those things which really makes America exceptional is the ability turning an idea into a profitable business in almost no time, while countries in Europe, Germany in particular, is undergoing long analytical processes before moving anything into action. This applies to renewable energy too.

Let's take solar energy as an example. While solar energy in Europe was triggered by the 'safe the planet' movement and heavily supported by energy laws and subsidies it were entrepreneurs in the United States who realized how profitable solar panels could be and that the government offered generous tax breaks.

Today, America is one of the biggest producers of solar energy, although only 1% of the U.S. energy derives from the power of the sun. The oldest solar power system in the world is located in California. Solar power is installed atop almost 200,000 homes with 650,000 photovoltaic panels across the United States. 10 years ago it were a mere 20,000 panels, a 30-fold increase[75].

---

[75] Source: Time Magazine, May 18, 2015

Looking at the states across America, particularly the sun soaked states Nevada, Arizona, Utah, New Mexico or Texas, where the sun shines almost year round, imagine what potential there is considering the millions of homes whose roofs could be plastered with solar panels and some vast, almost inhibited areas could be turned into huge solar farms. Of course this would also require huge investments storing the energy and transmitting it to cities where the energy is needed.

The governments of these states could make it even mandatory that solar panels have to be installed on all new homes. Subsidies and tax breaks are usually doing the trick getting builders motivated. May the sun be with you!

Movie Recommendations:
- *Duel in the Sun starring Gregory Peck*
- *Run for the Sun starring Richard Widmark*

57.　Water under the bridge

Over the span of a few million years, the Colorado River in the American west not only formed the Grand Canyon, it was and is the prime source of water in the states where the river runs through. The settlement and economic boom in the west would not had been possible without the water supply from the Colorado River.

In 1922, Arizona, California, Colorado, Nevada, New Mexico, Utah and Wyoming signed a contract to regulate the annual amount of water each state could take out of the river[76]. The contract also regulated the river level as basis for the annual take of water.

A few more things came into play. There is the fact that there was a lot of heavy rainfall in the years prior to the Colorado River Compound, lifting the water level in the river, on which the water allocation among the states was ruled in the contract. Unfortunately the region has not seen that much rain in any year since then. Added to that is the strong increase of the population, particularly in growth areas like Las Vegas or Phoenix. The huge settlement in the deserts with all its golf courses and swimming pools, which require loads of water, makes it important to manage water consumption in general and reducing the water take-out from the Colora-

---

[76] Source: Colorado River Compact, 1922 accessed on May 05, 2015

do River in particular. As one of the states using water from the Colorado River, California is hit more than just once. California is suffering from a drought dragging on for more than four years now. The itsy-bitsy rain fall every now and then only marks a drop on a hot stone.

The government of the Golden State in Sacramento was even forced to limit the water usage per head per day, which at first was hard to swallow for a population used to consume and waste natural water without any worries about conservation.

But then American innovation sets in and the people start to deal even with something uncommon like water shortage. Home owners in the desert South West are switching to desert landscaping, planting cactus instead of palm trees. Desert landscaping is also encouraged, promoted and supported by communities and in some stores you even find magazines catering to this innovative way of gardening.

Systems to desalinate, previously only known to the Middle East, are on the list of measures to escape the water shortage. Long term predictions regarding the needs, usage and waste of water are hard to make. Ten years ago probably nobody could have imagined that a state like California which received plenty of moisture in the Sierras and the San Francisco region could be plagued by a multi-year drought.

Other parts of the United States are getting a bit too much rain. May 2015 saw the heaviest levels of rain fall on record in Oklahoma, Arkansas or Texas. Like in other parts of the world, global warming brings severe weather to formerly ´dry´ desert states and heat waves to western mountainous states.

In winter, snow levels in the Rocky Mountains are the lowest since 500 reachs. Extreme cold temperatures are much less frequent than twenty or thirty years ago. Higher temperatures prevent the snow pack to stay on top of the mountains. In early spring the snow is melting away too early bringing fresh water to farm lands way before the crops are in the fields. Where there is shortage, there is business opportunity. Public water companies are increasingly subject to privatization and investors from near and far are filling their investment portfolios. Some sceptics say that the price of tab water could increase drastically and that at some point only the wealthy could afford clean drinking water.

According to some with a sense for paranoia and end-of-time phantasies believe, that a point could be reached in about 2025, when 40% of the population would have to acquire drinking water from private corporations. It is probably too early, flipping a coin on the likeliness[77].

Movie Recommendations:
- *Waterhole #3 starring James Coburn*
- *The Ballad of Cable Hogue starring mit Jason Robards*

---

[77] Source: Karen Piper: The Price of Thirst – Global Inequality and the Coming Chaos

58. Gone with the Wind

During my first trip through the American west in 1992 I drove from Los Angeles to Palm Springs and could not help but notice the huge number of windmills on the outskirts of Palm Springs. It was the first wind park I ever say but it was not the first wind park in the U.S. The first one was built in 1980 in New Hampshire. Shortly thereafter California started offering subsidies and tax breaks for operating wind mills.

The San Goronio Pass wind farm close to Palm Springs was erected in the 1980s and is still operated today. Palm Springs is known for its many golf courses and the location of even more retirement communities. Hollywood stars like Bob Hope helped establishing the city in the desert as a retirement place as well as weekend domicile for stressed people in the entertainment business.

In 1985, half of the energy produced from wind mills worldwide came from just one facility, the Altamont Pass farm in California. During the last 15 years, power obtained from wind parks increased 30-fold. Today, the U.S. are the 3rd largest producer of wind energy trailing only the European Union and China. About 4.5% of the energy produced in the United

States derives from wind energy[78]. The energy department has calculated that it would be possible covering 20% of the U.S. energy needs from wind power by 2030[79].

The weather patterns and the topography in states like North and South Dakota, Texas or Wyoming provide the perfect settings for wind park investments. Companies which only recently spent billions in oil exploration are switching to clean energy ventures now that oil prices are in free fall.

There is the example of an oil billionaire who intends to build a 3,000 megawatt wind mill in Wyoming. To get the power from the wind park to the big cities in Arizona, California or Nevada he also wants to erect a transmitting power line with a length of 1,000 kilometers[80]

---

[78] Source: Wikipedia: Wind power in the United States, accessed on July 10, 2015

[79] Source: U.S. Department of Energy

[80] Source: Handelsblatt, Page 64, Issue August 07, 2015

59. Black Gold

I n the 19th century, it was gold which lured adventurers and for-
tune hunters by the thousands into the west. It started off in California in 1848 and ended in the Black Hills of South Dakota towards
the end of the 19th century. In the 20th century fortunes were made with
black gold.

Shortly after Carl Benz produced the first car in 1885 triggering the
success stories of automobiles in Europe and the U.S., large scale entrepreneurs and small size wild cat operators, today they would probably be
called start-up companies, started drilling for oil in the United States.
They hit it big in California, Oklahoma and Texas.

The first small private oil well was operated in 1859 in the then territory of Oklahoma nearby Salina. The first commercial well followed 1889
in Chelsea and in 1896 a large oil field was detected in the vicinity of
Bartlesville. Before Oklahoma became a state in 1907 it was the world
largest oil producing region[81].

Texas was another pioneering U.S. state which was drilling for oil.
One of the first, big oil reservoirs was detected in 1901 in Spindletop near

---

[81] Source: Oklahoma Geology Notes, V. 62, No. 3, Fall 2002,accessed on July 03, 2015.

Beaumont. The oil industry transformed the state from a cattle country to an industry state during a very short period of time[82].

One of the corporate giants in the oil business was Standard Oil owned by John D. Rockefeller. At the turn of the century and way into the 1900s Standard Oil was a huge, powerful global conglomerate like Google or Amazon today.

The oil business remained on a high level until way after World War II. Increasing inexpensive oil production and the massive drilling in the Middle East and later on in South America made the oil industry in the United States less compatible.

At a time when the TV show Dallas occupied the top spots in the ratings around the globe, the Original that is, which showed a successful and profitable fictive oil dynasty, while the real oil producing industry in America was in decline.

This has changed again in the 21st Century. In the first ten years of this millennium drilling for oil became very profitable again while the oil prices climbed to new heights not seen since the oil crisis in the 1970s.

In 2013 the price for a barrel of oil peaked at USD 100 making expensive exploration methods profitable, particularly through vertical drilling, commonly known as fracking, in North Dakota and Texas.

---

[82] Source: Wikipedia, Texas Oil Boom, accessed on July 03, 2015

Fracking has turned parts of North Dakota from a thinly populated U.S. state where agriculture and cattle raising were the prime business into an oil bonanza, just like the gold rush did in South Dakota in the last quarter of the 19th Century. Within a short period of time some tiny towns became El Dorados of the oil industry.

As the oilfields are far from civilization on the vast prairie, the fracking fields look pretty similar to some gold camps in California during the rush in 1849. Oil workers receive top dollars for their work which is no surprise if the working conditions are considered and a production that operates 24/7.

The boom and the high oil prices also revived traditional oil exploration. Old wells which were abandoned in the 1980s when they became unprofitable are re-opened for business. There are plenty of small operations who are trying their luck drilling for liquid gold in some very rural places covered by rusty oil platforms where there is not much left but sagebrush. Up to 2014 the landscape close to Midland, Texas could have easily been taken for Saudi Arabia or Qatar.

Unfortunately the tides have changed again. The global financial crisis and the economic slow-down in China caused the oil prices to reach rock bottom. In the beginning of 2016 the price for a barrel of U.S. oil reached a new low at USD 27. As most modern drilling methods like fracking need up to USD 80 to produce a barrel of oil it is no surprise that many oil productions, especially those operating on depth, are going out of business or at least put their activities on hold till better times come around.

The low oil prices have a lot of advantages though. Energy prices for oil as well as for gas mean lower heating bills and more fun at the pump. Low energy prices are also a boost for the economy making American products affordable and compatible again. American companies, slowly but continuously are bringing manufacturing and industry production out-sourced to China and elsewhere back to the United States.

Movie and TV Recommendations:
- *Giant starring Rock Hudson*
- *Dallas starring Larry Hagman*
- *There will be Blood starring Daniel Day Lewis*

60. Desert in Flames

D o you remember the Flower Power time of the 1970s with flowers in the hair, free love and Woodstock? If there is anything comparable to the times back then it is the Burning Man Festival which is held every year from the end of August till early September in the Black Rock Desert in Nevada. Burning Man started 30 years ago.

At the first event, when it took place at Baker Beach, it is said that only 20 people participated. In 2014 70,000 were registered participants in Black Rock City[83].

It is not easy to describe what is happening there if you had not been there. If you are interested, ask previous participants or check out the photos and videos that can be found online. The fun starts with the arrival, because Black Rock City does not exist.

The city, if you want to call a camp with lots of tents and other bunking places a city, has to be built anew every year out of nothing and is being dismantled in such a thorough manner that travelers passing through

---

[83] Source: Wikipedia, Burning Man, accessed on June 03, 2015

in the weeks and months after the event can barely find any traces of the festivities.

The procedures include not letting water used for body washing just drip into the desert sand but to collect it and take it back to civilization. Taking about water, don´t expect and showers, swimming pools or running water. Besides all the attempts to protect the environment nature nevertheless gets some bruising.

The place in the desert in abandoned nature has to cope with the emissions from all those cars arriving in the middle of nowhere. As there is no water in Black Rock City huge quantities of bottled water have to be carried to the place in the desert, although those too are all being picked up after the event instead of being thrown away.

There also is an airport in Black Rock City, unfortunately without lounges for frequent flyers. A temporary landing strip is being paved allowing participants to fly in from the Reno-Tahoe airport in private jets or helicopters. The airstrip too is being paved away afterwards as it were never there. In 2009, 15,000 participants arrived by plane providing some insight that Burning Man is not just a gathering of environmental protectors and tree huggers.

Burning Man is also a place where the beautiful and the rich are gathered, although not necessarily from the A-list. They come to the desert to celebrate away from city lights and letting conventions and norms of the civilization, and quite often their clothes, behind during those festive weeks.

If you want to revive your memories of the 1970s and want to spend a summer vacation like back in Saint Tropez in the days of Brigitte Bardot, you may want to try it out. Ask your travel agent if Burning Man is right for you.

Movie Recommendations:
- *Three Godfathers starring John Wayne*
- *Desert Trail starring John Wayne*
- *Le Gendarme de St. Tropez starring Louis de Funés*
- *Bad Day at Black Rock starring mit Spencer Tracy*

List of References

George Draffan (1998): Taking back our land

Gustave Le Bon (1895): Psychologie der Massen

Karlheinz Moll (2014): FATCA – Wenn der Fiskus zweimal klingelt

Mike Lofgren (2012): The Party is over

Karen Piper (2014): The Price of Thirst

Michael F. Holt (1978): The Political Crisis of the 1850s

Gloria Jahoda (1995): The Trail of Tears

Steve Fischer (2005): When the Mob ran Vegas

Jim Hightower (2001): If the gods had meant us to vote, they would have given us candidates